The Cognitivity Paradox

The Cognitivity Paradox

*An Inquiry Concerning
the Claims of Philosophy*

BY JOHN LANGE

Princeton University Press 1970
Princeton, New Jersey

Foreword

As Russell might have said, this little book is not more original than it is. Beyond this I would say that many things in it have been suggested by or have an affinity with things said, or partly said, by a number of recent and contemporary philosophers. It has been bumped by Peirce's discussions of truth; and C. I. Lewis' Conceptualistic Pragmatism; and certain remarks by Carnap and Hempel, and Quine; and Roderick Chisholm's analysis of certain epistemic statements. I do not believe any of these men would accept all of what is said here, and I am sure that all of them would deplore that it is not said better. In the latter lamentation I concur.

Contents

The Cognitivity Paradox

one

Amiable Prolegomena

I have read the following little book with great interest, having written it. It has seemed to me, and it will undoubtedly seem to you, that it lacks most of the characteristics one has a right to expect of a professional performance. For example, it is not very neat; its limpidity is dubious; and it is not overly decisive. On the other hand the author, whom I have questioned closely on these matters, is while somewhat penitent not as apologetic as the canons of philosophical decency would seem to require. He has informed me that part of what the book is concerned with is the very notion of professional performance, particularly from the point of view of what one must presuppose in order that there be standards of professional performance. And to be sure, trying to speak of professional performance in a professional way without buying a certain set of criteria concerning professional performance is difficult. Probably because it is logically impossible.

I did mention it to the author that, in my opinion, this little book is more emotional than a philosophical essay should be, but he responded that he was not sure of that, and that was another one of those things the book was about. It seems to me then that this little book is about many things. Perhaps seldom in the history of philosophy has so small a book attempted to do so much and accomplished so little.

On the other hand I, for one, am willing to let people say what they want to say in the way they want to say it, though I admit that the maxim is somewhat revolutionary. If they want to say it loudly, I may wince, but I will allow them to do so. If they wish to be noisy, why not? After all, we are not running a library. And sometimes, the author informs me, people who yell are trying to say something. Indeed, that is why they are yelling, to let people know they are trying to say something. The author is of the unusual opinion that philosophy, like music and art, has upon occasion a right to be angry—say, hopping mad. It has this right, he insists, if there is good reason for anger; given such reason, he claims, somewhat repetitiously it seems to me, one has a right to be angry. Further, he asserts that to disguise this anger may be judicious subterfuge, but it is also deceit. I asked him if he thought that physics and chemistry have a right to be angry, but my only answer was a bewildered stare, from which I gather that the author does not believe that philosophy is physics and chemistry. I did take the liberty of pointing out to him that the fellow who yells may have nothing to say, and may just be yelling. He responded whether or not that is the case may easily be determined by listening, and perhaps that is true.

At this point I think I shall allow the author to speak for himself, and dissociate myself from his entire project.

two

Of Compasses and Gauntlets

This essay is addressed to the problem of the nature of philosophy, its cognitivity or lack of it. Perhaps many philosophers are already straight on this matter, but for myself and those who aren't, and for those who think they are, and aren't, a certain amount of unpleasant cogitation is in order. The essay is motivated by a number of things, but primarily perhaps by the difficulty of explaining to myself and others continuing philosophical disagreement, a phenomenon in our time overcome only in part by journal policies and hiring practices.

Perhaps the classical case in the philosophical clinic of the chronic worrier was Immanuel Kant, who, annoyed by perennial disagreement, sought to examine the limits and powers of human reason in philosophy's greatest attempt to establish a basis on which its cognitivity or lack of it might be delineated. As we know the result of his murky and magnificent analysis was a philosophical volcano that spewed forth more disagreement in the next two hundred years than the twenty centuries of relatively prosaic tumult it superseded.

The positivists too were upset by the vicious twaddle of purely verbal conflict, the solemn rhapsodies of metaphysicians whose profundity increased in direct ratio to the grammatical complexity of their utterances. Accordingly they set out to delimit and clarify the philosophical endeavor, dividing the world between the scientists and themselves. One of their passionate objectives was apparently getting philosophy in hand, refining it into something capable of judicious, exact treatment, making it something that an honest person could take seriously—determining its subject matter in such a way that one could be right or wrong, and others could find out.

A similar motivation might well seem to underlie the pseudopodic movements of ordinary language analysis. There in the linguistic habits of a given speech community, by fortunate coincidence the philosopher's, was a subject matter which was, at least within limits, empirically ascertainable. One can be right or wrong in assertions about how the expression 'free' is used, for example. One might then suppose that classical controversies might be resolved by examining how individuals use the expression 'free'. Of course, as it is now generally recognized by members of the movement, and was recognized several years earlier by nonmembers of the movement, how individuals use the expression 'free' is primarily relevant to the problem of how they use the expression 'free' and not to the classical controversies and problems to which philosophers had addressed themselves. On the other hand, as the ordinary language philosopher might point out, if that sort of thing is not relevant to the controversies over freedom, what is? That I think is a good challenge. In short, I see the commendable objective of the ordinary language analyst as the search for a criterion against which the correctness or incorrectness of philosophical assertions can be measured. That he finds this incredibly enough in ordinary language, almost always loosely and inadequately correlated with the comparative precision of experience, developed by nonphilosophers over hundreds of generations to deal with nonphilosophical problems and subserve nonphilosophical purposes, is less to be deplored than the fact is to be celebrated that he has honestly sought to find such a criterion. Many philosophers, it seems, have not done even that much. The ordinary language analysts, at least largely in the past, have sought, as did the Kantians and positivists, to establish the cognitivity of philosophy.

If we look across the Atlantic, or Channel, as the case may be, we can also see people concerned about cognitivity, about resolving disagreement. There perhaps introspection or intuition or some such unnerving methodology or nonmethodology is supposed to supply the criterion, and there again the fact that cognitivity is sought is more to be commended than the fact deplored that it is being sought in perhaps unlikely places.

Do we as philosophers not have a right to be embarrassed when we glance up into the stands, and notice the rest of the intellectual community gazing down at us in puzzlement, if not derision? They see us as costumed gladiators (some in white coats, some in smoking jackets, etc.) each defending his square yard of bloody sand against all comers. Is it any wonder if they ask themselves, "Are they trying to state truths, or are they just trying to kill each other?" And sometimes do we not, in a bothersome, twinging moment, probably at a philosophy convention, ask ourselves the same question?

three

Purposes, Strategies,
and Grumbles

Is philosophy cognitive? Can philosophy be
cognitive? What sort of things are philosophical
assertions? How do we go about finding if they
are true or not? Are they the sort of thing that
can be true or not? In general the question would
seem to be, "What are we as philosophers up to?"
This is in a sense to raise the old question which
we expect in Philosophy 1—"What is philosophy?"—and to which we give, judiciously, no
answer, or injudiciously, perhaps unworthily, one
of the stock answers from the shelf for contents to
be used in extinguishing student questions.

I am well aware that this question, or question-
complex, is not popular. In the past several years
it has been raised explicitly in extremely few journal articles, though several articles have responded
to it more or less directly, in the process of attend-
ing to more important questions. Ask yourself if
you can conceive of a dissertation committee ap-

proving such a topic. Ask yourself if a bright graduate student who knew the realities of the current philosophical market would dare to propose such a topic. The whole question seems to be one of those questions which endanger the digestion and are accordingly best left unasked.

But why should the question not be popular? Perhaps this is significant?

Are we afraid to ask this question, like the child who is afraid to open a door, because he is not sure what lies beyond it? I can remember once being advised, by a very fine philosopher, to worry less about analysis and more about doing some, and that is not a bad recommendation. On the other hand I see no reason why, say, "What is a philosophical question?" or "What sort of thing is a philosophical assertion?" is not itself a legitimate subject for consideration, if not for analysis. Surely it is worth thinking about, in some old-fashioned, nontechnical sense of the expression.

I wish to approach the question of the cognitivity of philosophy via a consideration of questions, predominantly philosophical questions, since if the nature of such questions could be clarified, then it seems one would be in a better position to assess the answers to such questions, and to determine whether or not the utterances proposed as answers to such questions could properly be said to be cognitive.

Specifically the next section of this essay is an attempt to examine several conceptions of the nature of philosophical questions. Perhaps not many of us will find these construals of the nature of the philosophical question that interesting or plausible, but I think we have heard most of them, and I have been given some of them by presumably well-intentioned people with whom I may not agree but who are undoubtedly qualified to form an opinion on the matter. Naturally I encourage other philosophers who might be interested in what they are doing, as well as in just doing it, to lend their efforts to supply more judicious characterizations of such questions.

Finally one must observe that it is surely the pervasive, if not unanimous, conviction of the philosophical community that philosophical assertions are cognitive, that they can be true or false, and that philosophical disagreement is genuine disagreement. We have all read the journals, undoubtedly not as much as we ought but probably more than we have genuinely liked. We see what is written there, our own articles and those of other philosophers. Those gray pages fairly steam of the conviction of cognitivity. Can we believe that Quine does not really believe he is pounding Carnap on the head, and that Carnap does not really believe he has dealt Quine a resounding blow? We find the most incredible assertions uttered with the casualness of an industrial chemist reading off the recipe for petroleum jelly. We find reviewers commenting on Jones' new book as though the reviewer were the *Logos* in disguise, an intolerable presumption were it not for the fact that the reviewer is, presumably, the *Logos* in disguise. We demolish one another with innocent and urbane aplomb and then are genuinely surprised that the other fellow does not catch on to the fact that he has been demolished. Our assurance, our astonishment, etc., is surely evidence of a sort that we regard what we are doing as cognitive.

Is it?

What is a philosophical question?

four

Consideration of
Selected Construals of the Nature
of Philosophical Questions

CONSTRUAL 1. *Question Q is a philosophical question if and only if it is a member of that class of questions whose members are the most general, pervasive questions the human mind can raise.*

This characterization is not altogether clear, but it is clear enough to see that it is incorrect. On the other hand the notion of generality frequently enters into the characterization of the philosophical question. Therefore it is worth pointing out that generality is neither a necessary nor a sufficient condition for a philosophical question.

That generality is not a sufficient condition for a philosophical question may be seen by examining the following set of questions:

Is this swan white?
Are all swans white?
Are all birds white?
Are all organisms white?

14

(Are the questions becoming more philosophical?)

Is everything that occupies time and space white?
Is all being white?

It seems these questions become increasingly general without becoming increasingly philosophical. Accordingly generality, even extreme generality, is not a sufficient condition for a philosophical question. Whether or not "Is being *qua* being white?" is a philosophical question I leave to the wild surmise of the reader.

Similarly generality is not a necessary condition for a philosophical question, since many philosophical questions discussed in journals are rather specific. Many critics of contemporary philosophy, we might note, deplore what they regard as the minute dimension of many problems considered recently in the literature. It seems to be their feeling that if the topics became any more specific they would disappear altogether.

CONSTRUAL 2. *Q is a philosophical question if and only if there is no settled answer to Q.*

Has one not heard that philosophical questions are to be distinguished by the fact that there are no settled answers to them—though perhaps their study may enlarge the mind, etc.? That this char-

15

acterization, vague like the former, is not judicious may be understood from the following observations.

Suppose the alarm clock rings again and there is a new revolution, or counterrevolution, in philosophy. All philosophers agree on answer A to classical problem P. In other words problem P is settled by agreement—we vote on it. Or let us say that we all agree that answer A is correct, proposed by, say, Herbert Feigl. Is classical problem P then no longer a philosophical problem? What counts as having a settled answer? Having an answer that would satisfy the *Logos?* Or just us, or 85 percent of the philosophical community, or what? Also of course there are many questions that do not have settled answers which are probably not philosophical questions at all, e.g., whether or not I should have the points in the automobile adjusted next month. Construal 2 has the unwelcome consequence that all unresolved questions qualify as philosophical.

But when people talk this way, they surely mean something more than the fact that certain questions do not *now* have settled answers. Presumably they intend to suggest that certain questions—philosophical questions—cannot have settled answers, ever, ever.

CONSTRUAL 3. *Q is a philosophical question if*

and only if it is a question to which no settled answer can be given.

CONSTRUAL 4. *Q is a philosophical question if and only if it is a question on which men are doomed to disagree eternally.*

These are romantic construals which those of us who are programmed for neatness are likely to find uninspiring.

If the third construal is correct, and no settled answers can be given to philosophical questions, we are faced with the historical paradox that philosophers on the whole have sought, often confidently, to give settled answers to these questions. In other words most philosophers do not believe Construal 3 is judicious, or presumably they do not understand what they are doing. Not many philosophers study philosophical questions because they enlarge the mind. Mind enlargement, if it occurs, is a by-product of philosophical inquiry, not its objective.

The fact that philosophers tend to reject certain answers to certain problems and the fact that they regard some solutions as better than others suggests that they believe there is a right answer to a problem, and the fact that they keep working suggests they believe this answer can be ascertained.

Construal 3 has the consequence, it should be

17

noted, that we do not know what questions are philosophical, in the particular case, unless we know which ones are not capable of receiving a settled answer. How would we know this? And if we knew it would we not stop working? Construal 3 suggests that philosophers are working only on what they believe to be nonphilosophical problems.

As in discussing Construal 2, one might ask: what counts as a settled answer? For example, let us suppose that all philosophers agree—at the American Philosophical Association convention, or at the meeting of the Aristotelian Society, or at some such conclave—that the solution to a certain philosophical problem is Herbert Feigl's A. The resolution to this effect is passed unanimously, and the philosophers then move on to a new unresolved problem. Presumably we would not settle philosophical questions by vote, but how would we settle them? Could we settle them by convincing one another that Herbert Feigl was *really* correct, or that C. D. Broad was, or some compromise candidate?

Can philosophical problems be solved by agreement? That is a more important question, I would guess, than it is likely to appear initially. The obvious "No-of-course-not!" answer, I suspect, tends to become less obvious the longer it is looked at. But if philosophical questions cannot be resolved by agreement, how can they be resolved? The scientist may have an answer to this, but I am not sure that we do. Perhaps one might want to say that the answer to a problem is that answer which need satisfy no finite set of philosophers but, in effect, the *Logos*. But do we believe that, or something like it—phrased perhaps in terms of the opinion to be fixed by an informed and rational community, assuming such a community would tend to a fixed opinion, if investigation could proceed indefinitely, etc.? Could even such ideal agreement settle philosophical problems? Also of course, given this approach, one would have no way of knowing what the ultimate agreement, or the opinion of the *Logos*, etc., would be.

Similar considerations are relevant to the fourth construal. For example, a question on which men did in fact terminate their disagreement would become *ipso facto* a nonphilosophical question, etc. Also of course, a nonphilosophical question on which men were determined to disagree, perhaps something having to do with the nature of light, or something along these lines, would, by this criterion, count as a philosophical question. So, too, for example, might many historical questions, pertaining, say, to the undiscoverable motivations and intentions of various historical figures, etc. Indeed, all questions to which settled answers could not be given, or all questions on which men were determined to "disagree eternally," would become philosophical questions—whether they were or not.

So much for Construals 3 and 4.

CONSTRUAL 5. *Q is a philosophical question if and only if it is a question philosophers concern themselves with.*

Construal 5 is pretty much a counsel of despair, and seems to be a way of saying—"Do what you want, and don't worry about whether or not it is philosophy in some unspecified sense." Construal 5 may be a felicitous recommendation, but it does not go far toward resolving the questions of this essay. In a way, it says, "Don't ask them."

It may be briefly shown to be injudicious by the consideration that many of the questions philosophers concern themselves with are not philosophical, e.g., "Where did I put the tire iron?", "Which fuse has blown out?", "When is the best time to plant grass seed?", etc.

CONSTRUAL 6. *Q is a philosophical question if and only if it is a question which philosophers concern themselves with in their professional capacity.*

I do not think Construal 6 is much good either, for several reasons, some of which might be briefly stated. For one thing, many philosophers concern themselves in their professional capacity with questions that are, presumably, nonphilosophical. For example, many philosophers are concerned with textual questions, with relatively scholarly questions pertaining to the works of other philosophers. For example, doing an expositional article or book does not seem to be primarily philosophical. Trying to figure out what Philosopher Jones meant does not seem to be a philosophical question; trying to find out why Professor Jones said what he did, or where he got the ideas for what he said, does not seem to be philosophical, etc. Similarly we can see philosophers concerned with delineating the use of certain expressions in a given speech community, a task which would appear to be descriptive and scientific, whether undertaken by scientists or not. For example, the gifted amateur astronomers of the nineteenth century were surely doing astronomy. It did not cease to be astronomy because they were amateurs. Beyond this it seems that some philosophers in our time have progressed well beyond the amateur phase and are actually doing acceptable linguistics. Indeed, in certain quarters I detect the sentiment that a young philosopher who has his wits about him would be well advised to be a linguist and not a philosopher, provided he concern himself with linguistics on a suitably abstract and theoretical level. And of course there are several philosophers working on problems that would seem to be mathematical rather than philosophical. For example, is theoretical work in mathematical logic philosophical work? If so, it seems we should say that many of the mathematical logicians in departments of mathematics are doing philosophy. Perhaps it is easier to say that many of the philosophers in departments of philosophy are doing mathematics?

But now let us suppose that all philosophers unanimously decide to devote their professional time to a consideration of some abstruse problem in physics, or civil engineering, and that the administrations of all the universities and colleges, rejoicing that philosophy has at last decided to bake some bread, to build some hardware, unite and bless this departure into applied empiricism. It would then be the case that all philosophers in their professional capacity would be considering a problem in physics or civil engineering. I do not think we would want to say then that a philosophical question can adequately be characterized as anything a philosopher, in his professional capacity, turns his hand to. This is not to deny that professional philosophers should be able to turn their hands to anything they like. It is only to deny that doing physics or civil engineering is doing philosophy, even if the physics and civil engineering is done by philosophers.

Perhaps at this point it should be noted that any of these construals *could be* regarded as purely stipulative, as merely laying down arbitrary criteria for the delimitation of philosophy. We can make 'All circles are square' an analytic statement if we wish, but there doesn't seem to be much point in doing so. What we are attempting to find is a likely, or relatively judicious, if not unexceptionable characterization of the philosophical question. We want to weave a net that will catch most philosophical questions and strain out most others. Perfection is not a property of most nets, but some nets are better than others.

Let us amend Construal 6.

CONSTRUAL 7. *Q is a philosophical question if and only if it is a question philosophers concern themselves with in their professional capacity provided it happens to be a philosophical question.*

Construal 7 is unilluminating in virtue of circularity and is a comment on Construal 6. Besides being unilluminating it is also incorrect. It makes the existence of philosophical questions depend on, among other things, the existence of professional philosophers. Presumably there were philosophical questions before there were professional philosophers or there would not have been anything to have been, or to pretend to have been, professional about. Moreover, even if all professional philosophers should somehow cease to exist, it seems probable that at least some philosophical questions

23

would not cheerfully agree to share their fate. These questions may need people but it is not clear they need professional philosophers. They might not get on as well without us, but they would undoubtedly get on. Most people consider some philosophical problems, at least at one time or another in their lives. And even our students occasionally surprise us, sometimes even those whom we regarded as possessing native gifts of a high order for obdurate and triumphant nonphilosophicality. Also of course there are presumably some questions which are philosophical which are no longer considered by professional philosophers and other questions which are philosophical which they have not yet considered, and perhaps never will.

CONSTRUAL 8. *Q is a philosophical question if and only if it occurs on List L.*

Suppose that philosophy is a big room filled with various sorts of furniture. The furniture has been in this room for a long time. We are then asked to characterize the furniture in the room. How would we do it—distinguishing it from the furniture in other rooms? And is everything in the room its furniture? What about the glass in the window, the rugs on the floor, the pictures on the wall? Rather than look for a generic characteristic, or something of that sort, we might well be tempted to prepare an inventory of the room's contents—basing this inventory on our acknowledged familiarity with the room. We might then list everything that has traditionally been in the room, whether it is normally regarded as furniture or not. It seems this attack on the problem might well be more successful than the attempt to specify a generic characteristic for the room's furniture. What if the only generic characteristic of the room's furniture was that it was the room's furniture?

Construal 8 seems to presuppose that we have a pretty good idea of what philosophical questions are like—after all, we bump into them everyday, read about them, worry about them, etc.—but that we find it extremely difficult to determine a nontrivial generic characteristic, or at least to state one. Accordingly it recommends that we prepare a list and characterize the philosophical question in virtue of its presence on the list.

Before we righteously denigrate this proposal we might ask ourselves if this is not what in effect we normally do—for example, in classes, in anthologies of philosophy, etc. If we want to throw stones at this proposal, we should at least be aware that most of us must throw them from the inside of our own glass houses. Actually a given philosopher is not likely to find this proposal too unattractive, provided he is guaranteed that he can draw up the list. It is letting Plato or St. Thomas or

25

Heidegger or Rudolf Carnap draw up the list that is likely to worry us.

Perhaps the crucial difficulty with the list approach is that the criterion for placement on the list is not clear. How do we determine that a problem goes on the list or not? How would we resolve disagreement? The list, to be adequate, would seem to presuppose an intuitive criterion, and the intuitive criterion is what we would really like to find. Without that how would we know if the list were correct or not? How would we know whether a new problem which occurs to someone is to be placed on the list or not? The list approach might be genuinely helpful as a step toward clarifying the notion of a philosophical problem, but it can hardly resolve that problem itself.

CONSTRUAL 9. *Q is a philosophical question if and only if it resembles Paradigm Question P.*

Similar objections to those proposed as relevant to Construal 8 are, it would seem, relevant to this proposal, so it will not be discussed in detail. As stated, at least, this proposal seems to be considerably narrower than Construal 8, although much here depends on the capacity of the individual to note relevant resemblances among problems. The list approach, of course, might be construed along the lines of being a multiple paradigm approach.

26

But here, as with the list, there seems to be no effort to *find* the property in virtue of which the paradigm *is* a philosophical question, and that property, if there is one, is surely the desideratum of inquiry—or else the desideratum is to make it plausible that there is *no such property*. On the paradigm approach, of course, it would now be stipulated that there *is* such a property or set of properties, namely, *resemblance to the paradigm*. The paradigm itself then becomes a philosophical question, it would seem, not because it is philosophical but because it resembles itself, which would be hard to deny. Also of course this construal does not offer a criterion for recognizing *relevant* common traits among problems (almost all questions will resemble one another in several ways) or a criterion for recognizing degrees of what might be spoken of as "relevant resemblance." This approach would seem to be the counsel of armchair mysticism. Also of course we might be concerned with who gets to choose the paradigm problem.

CONSTRUAL 10. *Q is a philosophical question if and only if it is one of the most profound or significant questions the human mind can ask.*

I think there are many philosophers who buy, or come close to buying, this construal although they would probably be horrified to see it stated

27

so bluntly. This construal, on the other hand, like its predecessors, will not do the job of characterizing the philosophical question. For example, surely there are extremely profound and significant nonphilosophical questions. If we do not wish to regard certain scientific questions, having to do with, say, the nature or the origin of the solar system, as profound or significant, surely we must recognize thousands of moral questions as being of the most urgent importance, so much so that it would be farcical not to recognize their profundity and significance. And let it not be said that these questions are less profound than, say, questions in metaethics, because the metaethical questions are logically prior. Rather it might be said that the metaethical questions obtain whatever urgency they might have, if any, derivatively, that it is the profundity and significance of the moral questions which provide whatever importance might attach to them. Were it not for the moral issues involved, the metaethical questions would not be much more than classroom exercises, just so much more philosophical doodling. Correspondingly, just as there are profound and significant nonphilosophical questions, so presumably there are nonprofound and nonsignificant philosophical questions. At least some critics of contemporary philosophy have suggested that this is the case, and perhaps they are correct. I shall not hazard any examples for fear that some philosopher would regard them as profound and significant. At any rate, even if all philosophical questions currently discussed were indeed profound and significant, one supposes that profundity and significance might be accompanying rather than defining characteristics of such problems, just as it may be the case that a consistent and complete logistic system is dear to all logicians, or piety is dear to all the gods, without its being the case that being the object of the devotion of logicians or having the respect of the gods *makes* things complete and consistent logistic systems or pious. In support of this supposition, one might note that even if all philosophical questions under current discussion were, per hypothesis, profound and significant, it seems it would still be possible to *invent* a philosophical question which was neither, and this possibility alone suffices to destroy any plausibility which might have attached to Construal 10.

CONSTRUAL 11. *Q is a philosophical question if and only if it is a question of logical or linguistic analysis.*

This is obviously a proposal as to what philosophy should be and not an account of what philosophy used to be, is, or must be. It is a recommenda-

29

tion to philosophers rather than a description of philosophy, so we need not discuss it in detail. It will be enough to point out that many questions philosophers concern themselves with cannot be understood as questions of linguistic analysis, and that not all questions of linguistic analysis are philosophical questions. In the first case, one need not have recourse to extinct species of metaphysician but may simply refer to much of what goes on on the Continent, in phenomenological and existential philosophy. In the latter case, one might ask oneself if one would regard the following questions as philosophical: "What do we mean by 'doughnut'?" "What is the ordinary use of 'turnip'?" "What is the logic of the expression 'machine bolt'?" (Or perhaps to be more up to date, "What is the logical geography of the set of concepts pertaining to machine bolts?") On the other hand, should the preceding questions be indubitably philosophical, though perhaps not of great interest, it would still be the case that meeting this criterion was not a necessary condition for a philosophical question. And of course, from my point of view, it would not seem sufficient either. If I am unable to think up a question in linguistic analysis which is not philosophical, perhaps the exponent of the view can. For example, is the linguist who tries to understand the functioning of an expression in Bassa doing philosophy?

30

CONSTRUAL 12. *Q is a philosophical question if and only if it is a question of analyzing presuppositions.*

This construal may be disregarded because there are philosophical questions which do not analyze presuppositions and questions which pertain to the analysis of presuppositions which are not philosophical. Admittedly the notion of "analyzing presuppositions" is pretty vague, but I do not believe that I invented its vagueness. For example, any attempt to discover what is entailed by what *might* be construed as an analysis of presuppositions, but I think this is not what is normally meant. For example, doing problems in the propositional calculus is not normally construed as analyzing presuppositions. Similarly, tracing the connections among concepts in, say, deontic logic, does not seem to be analyzing presuppositions, though it seems to be doing philosophy.

On the whole I think it is unclear just what analyzing presuppositions involves. For example, it is one thing to analyze the presuppositions of a statement S, in the sense of attempting to discover what the speech environment must be like for it to be meaningfully uttered; and another to assert that a form of intuition must be presupposed to account for a certain character of experience; and another to assert that "science" presupposes the concept of causality, or something of that sort.

31

Consider the case of the presuppositions of science. This vague topic might be construed as the attempt to discover the *de facto* convictions without which scientists would not do their work as they do, in which case it seems clearly a case for the clinical psychologist; or it might be understood as the attempt to discover the logically necessary conditions for an enterprise to exist, in which case a category mistake appears to have taken place, and the road to mysticism and metaphysics looms ahead; or it might be understood as the attempt to propose something in the nature of a rational reconstruction of certain aspects of the scientist's work, for example, proposing a model of scientific explanation, or something along these lines, in which case one model must presumably compete with another model, and the criteria for evaluating models are not completely determined by descriptive accuracy. In the latter sort of case, incidentally, one might well speak not so much of the *analysis* of presuppositions as, if one wishes to speak of presuppositions at all, the *proposal* of presuppositions—which it might be well for the scientist to presuppose, but which in fact he might not.

Correspondingly of course we would not allow all analyses of presuppositions to count as philosophy, or at least I would suppose not. For example, the analysis of the presuppositions of Japanese gardening, milk bottle design, Jones' bridge play-

ing, etc., would presumably not count as philosophical.

I THINK it is clear that none of the preceding
twelve construals provides an adequate characterization of the nature of philosophical questions. On
the other hand I think they are not, or most of
them, altogether unfamiliar to us. I have not just
invented them; they are not just random proposals.
They, or many of them, are the sorts of things
that are often said about philosophical questions,
and they seem to be all wrong. Then what is right?

It is surely extremely difficult to develop an adequate characterization of the philosophical question, and I encourage other philosophers to think
about this. It is, of course, not an attractive object
of philosophical inquiry because it is messy to the
point of being comparatively impervious to the
contemporary desideratum of clarity. This fact
alone informs us that many of the best philosophers
of our day will not consider it. It is further unattractive because its serious consideration might lead
to a revision of one's conceptions of the nature,
scope, and power of philosophy. And philosophers
do not take to reconsidering basic commitments
any more happily than any other, in the final
analysis, human being.

My suspicion is that an adequate general construal of the philosophical question may be impossible, but I find this counterintuitive, because I feel that I, and others, can and do, with a fair amount of ease and a high degree of consistency, separate philosophical from nonphilosophical questions. How we do this I am not sure, but that we can do it seems obvious. It seems plausible there may be some elusive criterion to be discovered.

Compatible with this hypothesis is the observation that many of the above construals, even if individually inadequate, do as a matter of fact include many philosophical questions, if not all, and do exclude many nonphilosophical questions, if not all. This might suggest that some complex property should be the object of inquiry, or, to put this in the linguistic mode, that some conjunction or disjunction of construals, say, those above, might be plausible.

This proposal may be ruled out, however, given the observation that if none of the construals individually states a necessary condition for a philosophical question, then no disjunction nor conjunction, or other truth-functional combination of construals, could count as a necessary condition, other than in the trivial sense that a logical combination of construals into the form of a tautology would be a *necessary condition* for the truth of any statement to the effect 'Q is a philosophical question'.

For example, 'It is raining or it is not raining' is a necessary condition for the truth of all statements whatsoever, e.g., 'Some dogs bite', because it is entailed by all statements. Similarly 'Q either meets Construal 1 or it does not' would be a necessary condition for the truth of any statement to the effect 'Q is a philosophical question'. But it is also of course a necessary condition for the truth of 'Some dogs bite' and all other statements, including its own negation. Analogously a truth-functional combination of construals which was inconsistent would be a *sufficient condition* for the truth of 'Q is a philosophical question', because an inconsistent statement entails that statement, along with all other statements, including, say, 'Some dogs bite', and its own negation. Noting these facts we observe that it is simple to produce both sufficient and necessary conditions for the truth of any statement to the effect 'Q is a philosophical question', but somehow the inquiry does not seem far advanced. This is an instance of knowing necessary and sufficient conditions for the truth of 'Q is a philosophical question' and not knowing anything about philosophical questions.

At this point perhaps the following objection to our procedure should be considered: "The 'if-and-only-if' approach to these matters is a mistake. It presupposes there is a generic property, of whatever complexity, which there is not. What one is better advised to do is to attempt to list 'family resemblances,' etc."

This may be a quite good objection, but there are some things to be said about it. First, the claim that there is no generic property of philosophical questions is a negative existential hypothesis, which would be entailed by no consistent finite set of evidence-statements. Accordingly, whereas it is theoretically possible that I should establish that there is a generic property of philosophical questions, namely, by finding one, it is not theoretically possible to establish that there is no such property. If I can produce a centaur, I show that centaurs exist. The fellow who claims centaurs do not exist cannot prove his point by producing any finite number of noncentaurs, e.g., ink wells, horses, philosophical articles, etc. On the other hand, of course, it may well be that there are no centaurs. To discuss this point fully involves numerous related questions, for example, whether or not we can *know* a particular existential statement to be true. A consideration of these questions, however, lies beyond the scope of this little book. Secondly, if there is no generic property of philosophical questions, it is not clear how we will make plausible the claim that there is none except by following the procedure of this paper, or one similar. Surely one cannot just start out by assuming there is no generic property. Nor does one find it easy to just "look and see" that there is none. It takes a lot of looking and seeing, and it still seems to be that there may well be some such property. How does the objector know that there is not? He takes faster looks? Thirdly, if there is such a generic property, we are not likely to find it by assuming that it does not exist. We are better entitled to assume that it does not exist after we have looked very hard for it, and have failed. Fourthly, the if-and-only-if approach allows us to reject a number of mistaken construals. If it cannot show us what is right, it provides at least a test for eliminating some of the things which claim to be right. Precision should be pushed as far as possible. There is no point in blurring edges until we get to the place where the edges are blurred. I had rather invent an edge than miss one that exists. Inventing edges is undoubtedly a philosophical fault, but pretending they do not exist is not obviously more virtuous.

At any rate—whatever the value of the preceding pages of argumentation—they should make clear at least that the nature of the philosophical question is not clear. This is perhaps not an astonishing conclusion, but once it is admitted—REALLY ADMITTED—then the problems involved in instituting or understanding claims of cognitivity in philosophy suddenly emerge into a most obnoxious prominence. Today philosophy sits on a tack, and it is up to us either to remove the tack or go and sit down somewhere else. We could also continue to sit on the tack, but that hurts. Especially after one notices that one is sitting on it. It is probably best of course not to have noticed, but after one has noticed it is hard not to have noticed, and after one has noticed, one is, so to speak, stuck.

five

Classification and
Nonclassification Questions

I would now like to distinguish between two
major sorts of questions, and then to distinguish
between two sorts of questions within one of the
major divisions. I have found it difficult to develop
a terminology to mark these distinctions, but the
following approximates what I have in mind.

1. Nonclassification questions
2. Classification questions
     (1) with true/false answers possible
     (2) with better/worse answers possible

This terminology is inadequate for various reasons, probably including several of which I am un-
aware. One difficulty is of course that perhaps most
questions, if not all, could be construed as, in a
sense, classification questions. For example, "Do
tigers eat meat?", which I would regard as an example of a nonclassification question, could be regarded as a question to the effect, "Should tigers

be classified among meat-eating animals?" Similarly "Should I go to the movie tonight?" might be rephrased, "Should my going to the movie tonight be classified among the acts I should do?", etc.

The sort of thing I am trying to get at is the distinction between those questions where the classificatory scheme is being *merely applied*, and those in which the scheme itself is under consideration. For example, if we ask "Do tigers eat meat?" we assume we are clear on the notions of tigers and meat eating, and we merely wish to find out if tigers do, as a matter of fact, eat meat. On the other hand questions such as "What sorts of things are tigers?" and "What counts as being a meat eater?" would be classification questions. They are questions pertaining to the classificatory scheme and not to its application.

I think that the distinction, so understood, between the classification and the nonclassification question is relevant to the distinction between the philosophical and the nonphilosophical question, though it does not appear to be the same distinction.

For example, there are classification questions we would not regard as philosophical, and there are, perhaps, philosophical questions we would not regard as classification questions. For example, the classification question "What sorts of things are machine bolts?" is not a philosophical question, and the nonclassification question "Is there a Divine Entity?" has been, traditionally at least, a question regarded as philosophical—or at least it has been a question to which philosophers have conscientiously addressed themselves. My own feeling with respect to the latter question is that it is not particularly judicious to regard it as a philosophical question, but rather that one might perhaps better say that it presupposes philosophical questions which, once clarified, might transform it into either a pseudo-question or a question of existential fact, which we might be unable to resolve but which we might be able to consider rationally in the light of empirical evidence.

Even though the distinction between the classification and the nonclassification question is not the same distinction as that between the philosophical and the nonphilosophical question, I think it illuminates the latter distinction. It seems to me that most philosophical questions are concerned with the adequacy or inadequacy of a classificatory scheme, or are concerned to propose a classificatory scheme in order to systematize and interpret some set of data, perhaps a set of linguistic practices, perhaps a tangle of disturbing concepts having to do with responsibility and empirical law, perhaps having to do with our sensory, moral, or aesthetic experience of the world.

It may be noted that I do not contend that philosophy is concerned with *explanatory* schemes, for a necessary condition for an explanatory scheme, in my opinion, is that it should yield empirically testable prediction-statements, an accouterment fortunately not expected of classificatory schemes and I hope not of philosophy. This is not to claim, of course, that any scheme which does yield empirically testable prediction-statements is an explanatory scheme, for one might put prediction-statements in a hat and prescribe a procedure for their withdrawal, and so produce a scheme that would yield prediction-statements, but still not have anything that could be called an explanation, presumably even if the prediction-statements invariably turned out to be true. Similarly it should be admitted that the amorphous nature of explanatory *matrices*, or theory *matrices*, such as the Sapir-Whorf linguistic relativity thesis, Marxist theory, Freudian psychology, Spengler's and Toynbee's theories of history, etc., blurs the otherwise too neat distinction between the classificatory and the explanatory scheme. Theory matrices may be the stuff of which theories are made, but until the theory matrix is rigorized, it is usually not even clear what the prediction-statements of the theory matrix are. A theory matrix might, ideally, be rigorized by specification of vocabulary, determination of formation and transformation rules, selection of axioms, and the formulation of designation rules, in short, by constructing a correspondent interpreted axiomatic system. If one is not clear on what prediction-statements are *entailed* by a theory matrix, the relevance of a false prediction-statement to the plausibility of the theory matrix is difficult to assess. Indeed, given the vagueness and nonsystematicity of most theory matrices, one might be well advised not to speak of what prediction-statements the theory matrix entails, but of what prediction-statements it *suggests*. Presumably in the theory which is constructed to correspond to the original theory matrix these prediction-statements, only suggested in the original matrix, would, among many others, actually be derivable as theorems. Sometimes the persistent rejection of putative counterevidence to a theory matrix suggests that the appearance of empirical content in the theory matrix may be deceptive and that its defenders have perhaps transformed it unbeknownst to themselves into tautology. If so, the theory matrix would not constitute an explanatory scheme. One might speak here of the challenge of systematicity. Sometimes matrices will respond well to the challenge and they, or parts of them, will become science; sometimes the challenge is not met and the theory matrix is revealed as only metaphysics, gobbledygook, or perhaps philosophy. This embarrassment, or demotion, of course, is inflicted only on those philosophies which have injudiciously proposed themselves as being explanatory schemes. Philosophy can tell of the world, but it cannot explain it. This is all right. Let us remain calm. Prediction-statements need not be the sole interest of the rational mind nor their presence the index to intellectual achievement.

Within the classification questions I should like to separate out those to which true/false answers may be given and those to which only better/worse answers may be given. Some questions intrinsically pertaining to a classificatory scheme presumably have true/false answers. This would seem to be the case, for example, when one aspect of the classificatory scheme can be determined in virtue of another aspect of the scheme, or in virtue of another scheme which is provisionally accepted. For example, "Is the class of centaurs a subclass of the class of mythological creatures?" would appear to be a question pertaining to a classificatory scheme, and it surely has a true/false answer. It is not altogether clear in this instance whether one would want to say the classificatory scheme is merely being applied, or is itself under consideration. In a sense it is merely being applied, but to itself, in a sense it is itself under consideration.

I think it is obvious, however, that the most interesting classification questions are those which *cannot be resolved* by semantic transformation and deductive logic but require a certain element of creativity or imagination—questions which require classificatory hypothesis, which involve the invention of an intellectual grid or the construction of a conceptual framework for ordering the domain under consideration. It is important to note, in questions of this sort, that significant agreement on data, on some level, is normally presupposed and that the job is primarily to organize and interpret the data in what seems to be the most illuminating and systematic fashion. Presumably one adjudicates questions like these on grounds of utility, not of truth or falsity. There is of course the recurrent temptation to say that the most satisfying hypothesis must be the true hypothesis, but how would one know that? Does it even make sense to claim that one knows it? How would one prove that one knew it? Is "satisfaction" somehow essentially involved in the meaning of 'true'? It does not seem essentially involved in the meaning of 'true' when one discusses the truth value of 'Dogs are animals' or 'Some dogs bite'.

To illustrate this matter, let us suppose that we confront our own moral experience and what we can gather of the moral experience of others. We might then propose to ourselves questions concerning the cognitivity of our moral convictions and ask ourselves whether the most illuminating interpretation, the most satisfying interpretation of the data, is in terms of, say, a cognitivist or a noncog-

45

nitivist metaethic. In considering this matter it is of extreme importance to note, though it is almost never noted, that a given set of data will be compatible with a variety of accounts which are at least verbally incompatible with one another. Putting this matter in another way, one might point out that it is possible to construct verbally incompatible premise-sets which will generate the same set of statements. Let us suppose that 'q' is a statement. Then it would be possible to construct an infinite number of verbally incompatible premise-sets which would entail 'q'.

I would now like to introduce and explicate two expressions, 'data-"statement"' and 'data-statement'. A data-"statement" is a linguistic entity which *is* data for interpretation or explanation; a data-statement is a *statement* which *reports* or *describes* data for interpretation or explanation. In 'data-"statement"' I place quote marks on 'statement' in order to refer neutrally to linguistic entities which from the logical point of view might be either statements (linguistic entities with truth values) or pseudo-statements (linguistic entities which have the grammatical form of a statement but which are not statements in the logical sense, i.e., they are not linguistic entities possessing truth values).

Some problems connected with these notions might be illustrated in the following manner. Suppose that we have a beaker of fluid and the fluid turns green, and that we wish to explain this. We might then report the data to be explained by the data-statement 'This liquid turned green'. On the other hand suppose the liquid turns green and a bystander utters the following observation 'This liquid is immoral'. Presumably his observation is *not* a data-statement. This is not to claim that 'This liquid is immoral' is nonsense, but only that it is not to be considered a data-statement, for reasons shortly to be specified. One attractive construal of 'This liquid is immoral' might be that it is logically false, for it is analytic that only moral agents can be immoral, and it is analytic that liquids cannot be moral agents; accordingly its negation, 'This liquid is not immoral', would be logically true. On the other hand I do not favor this proposal because I do not think it is analytic that liquids cannot be moral agents, at least if we understand 'moral agent' as meaning 'entity which can be moral or immoral'. I would like to think that we can conceive of what it would be for a liquid to be conscious, sloshing about its beaker, turning green, etc., and could conceive that it might harbor immoral thoughts, perhaps envying other liquids their larger beakers or better vantage points on the laboratory shelves. This is not much different from imagining that Jones, whose behavior we observe, has a mind. Accordingly I would suppose the best construal

47

of 'This liquid is immoral' is that it is empirically false; and that its negation, 'This liquid is not immoral', is empirically true, for the probabilities are that liquids are not conscious, and even if they were conscious it might well be the case that they were quite moral. But in any case 'This liquid is immoral' is not a data-statement, nor would be its negation. My primary reason for refusing to call 'This liquid is immoral' a piece of nonsense is that it seems to me to be *false*, and falsity, like truth, is a sufficient condition for significance.

As I use the expression 'data-statement' we should, *intersubjectively*, be capable in principle of establishing or confirming the truth of a data-statement via observation. This is not to alter the meaning originally assigned to 'data-statement' but to clarify the presupposed restriction on what may count as *data* in virtue of which 'This liquid is immoral' is not regarded as a data-statement. If restricting the application of the expression 'data' to that which is intersubjectively ascertainable in principle by observation seems too extreme, one might propose a distinction between intersubjective and subjective data, or something of that sort, and then suitably distinguish between data-statements of correlated types. However, for the purposes of this essay, I shall understand 'data' to be applicable only to *intersubjective* phenomena, with corresponding consequences for the notion of the data-statement.

Whether or not this is a judicious restriction will be argued shortly.

Accordingly 'Jones has a mind' would not count as a data-statement, though presumably it is a true statement; and data-statements would lend plausibility to its truth claim. Similarly 'This liquid is immoral' would not be a data-statement, though presumably it possesses a truth value and data-statements would be relevant to the supposition of its truth or falsity. A data-statement that lends plausibility to the claim that 'This liquid is immoral' is false is 'This is liquid', for, as far as we know, liquids lack several of the properties with which moral potentiality tends to be associated, for example, the possession of physiological sensors and a central nervous system. Of course angels presumably lack physiological sensors and a central nervous system, too. If there are angels, and they do lack physiological sensors and a central nervous system, then it would seem plausible to suppose that angels, too, are not moral agents, or perhaps rather that the case for the moral potentialities of liquids is thereby considerably strengthened.

As I use 'data-statement' then, 'Jones has a mind' would not be a data-statement, but 'Jones sneezed' would. This use of 'data-statement' of course requires consideration, for example, with respect to the notion of what is observable in principle and with respect to the advisability of its restrictiveness.

For example, Jones' statement 'I, Jones, have a headache', which presumably does *not* mean 'I, Jones, am wrinkling my forehead, squinting my eyes, uttering aggrieved sounds, etc.', would not count as a data-statement since the phenomenon it reports is not intersubjectively observable. Perhaps then one should speak of enlarging the notion of data-statement to include introspective reports, or assertions pertaining to private conditions, but then it would be difficult to avoid counting as data-statements such claims as 'That polar bear has a headache', 'That amoeba has a headache', 'That liquid has a headache', etc. I think the notion of a data-statement is clear enough for what we are doing here, but it is admittedly a notion that deserves, and will not receive, further consideration, at least in this context.

One attendant reason for the restrictions placed on the use of 'data-statement' is that I want data-statements to refer to something which can, by all competitive explanations or interpretations, be taken to be *that which is to be explained* or *that which is to be interpreted*. If one cannot even agree on *what* is to be explained or interpreted, the hope for either explanation or interpretation would seem to be foredoomed. Earlier I spoke of the adjudication of classificatory schemes normally presupposing significant agreement on data, and these proposals with respect to 'data' and 'data-statement' are intended to mark out at least one type of phenomena on which, if on no others, significant agreement might well be supposed.

Granting that 'This liquid is immoral' is not a data-statement, i.e., it does not report or describe data for interpretation or explanation, one might note that it itself is surely of some interest. If we are psychologists, we might be interested in the *actual* data-statement 'The bystander said 'This liquid is immoral' ', which *is* a report of data to be explained within the context of psychological theory; if on the other hand we are philosophers, we might not be interested so much in the data-statement 'The bystander said 'This liquid is immoral' ' as in the data-"statement" itself, namely, the linguistic entity uttered: 'This liquid is immoral'. Analogously much attention in metaethics, sometimes exclusive attention, is devoted to data-"statements", i.e., linguistic entities taken as themselves data for interpretation or explanation.

Concentrating on the data-"statements" of ethics is to approach, hopefully not to evade, moral experience via the language which is associated with such experience. It seems to me that such an approach is often peculiarly judicious. On the other hand it would be unfortunate if the linguistic approach were regarded as an exclusive avenue into the understanding of moral phenomena, the nature of which is more likely to be ascertained by con-

51

fronting a moral problem than by examining sentences containing normative predicates. Surely it must be admitted that what gives the data-"statements" of ethics their significance is the convictions they reflect, the moral earthworks from which they spring, the moral matrix without which their utterance would be little more than arbitrary and incomprehensible disturbances in the larynx; nonetheless they, unlike the tortured sediment that generates them, are relatively accessible to inquiry. One sentence written on the blackboard is usually more helpful than a truckload of moral sensitivity. Although the phenomenology of normative experience is undeniably richer than the language that emerges out of it, the battles of cognitivity are presumably most suitably fought on the linguistic level.

Now let us regard a given linguistic entity 'q', which we shall suppose to be a data-"statement" of ethics to the effect that random slaughter of members of the in-group is seldom morally praiseworthy. Now we might believe that 'q' is true, or we might believe that it is false, or we might be agnostic on the matter, or we might suppose that it lacks a truth value altogether. If we took any of the first three positions, we would be cognitivists; if the last, noncognitivists. But let us focus on the first and fourth alternatives, and speak simply of the first as being the cognitivist's and the fourth as being the noncognitivist's position. Presumably both the cognitivist and the noncognitivist are interested in generating 'q', the first believing 'q' to be true and the latter, while denying it a truth value, acknowledging that it is a verbal formula subscribed to in the community, uttered frequently, etc. This being the case, the cognitivist and the noncognitivist can both construct premise-sets which will generate 'q'. Instead of speaking of premise-sets, let us now suggest that both the cognitivist and the noncognitivist could divise an ethical theory which would generate 'q'. These theories presumably would be divergently structured or, at least, divergently interpreted; surely at least their associated metatheories would be verbally incompatible, for in one 'q' would be understood to be true and in the other it would be understood to lack a truth value; but both theories would entail 'q'. This result could of course be multiplied for data-"statements" 'r', 's', 't', etc. Thus both the cognitivist and the noncognitivist theories would be compatible with the data in the strong sense that the desired data-"statements" would be logical consequences of the theory.

It should be noted at this point that neither theory, as here conceived, would be an *explanatory* scheme in the sense previously developed; the analogy would be to a geometrical and not a physical theory. The developed theorems would not be prediction-statements, the presence of which is necessary to an explanatory scheme in the sense previously discussed. Admittedly 'explanation' is a severally ambiguous expression, e.g., 'I shall explain the meaning of a word', 'I shall explain the route to Albany', 'I shall explain why I do not have the term papers graded', 'I shall explain his motives', etc., but 'explanation' in the sense that it is used in 'explanatory scheme' is explanation which yields empirically testable prediction-statements as, for example, one might expect in astronomy or physics. Given the ambiguity of 'explanation', it would not violate English, a usefully tolerant tongue, to speak of the cognitivist and the noncognitivist theories as being "explanations" of data, but I think this would be somewhat confusing, and it is much clearer to speak of them as *interpretations* or *accounts* of the data. This is not to deny that it might be possible to develop an explanatory theory, say, a theory in psychology, from which it might follow that a given individual under certain circumstances might *utter* 'q'.

If, as we shall suppose, our cognitivist and our noncognitivist theories are equally compatible with the data, entailing the same set of desiderated data-"statements", then the decision between the two theories—our decision as to which theory to accept—must presumably be made on *independent* grounds, the adjudication presumably being determined in virtue of such considerations as simplicity, systematicity, aesthetic attractiveness, or moral import. Yes, moral import. On the other side of the ledger it cannot be denied that there is a certain schizophrenic charm in embracing an immoral theory at a suitably abstract level while in practice devoting oneself earnestly to worthy endeavors, redoubling as though in compensation one's efforts to bring about a more just state of affairs in the world, etc. If it weren't for the fact that most noncognitivists have such high moral standards, the theory would be more objectionable than it is. There is something playful about noncognitivism, and this is perhaps one of the attractions of the position—that it is so innocent that no one would dream of taking it seriously. On the other hand, if it tended to be a nomological consequence of embracing noncognitivism that the moral agent who did so thereby became increasingly moral, then this might be a good reason for embracing the theory.

six

First-order and
Second-order Philosophy

I would now like to distinguish between what I might, with admitted tendentiousness, call first-order philosophical questions and second-order philosophical questions.

First-order philosophical questions will be classification questions which do not, at least *prima facie*, admit of true/false answers. Second-order philosophical questions will be classification questions which do admit of true/false answers. What I am doing here, of course, is *not* attempting a general explication of the notion of philosophical question, a notion which I suppose we all have in one degree of obscurity or another, but drawing attention to certain types of philosophical questions. Presumably there are philosophical questions, or questions regarded traditionally as philosophical, which are neither first- nor second-order questions in the above senses. Also of course, as pointed out earlier, there are classification questions of both sorts which are not philosophical questions. On the other hand it is my surmise that what I call first-order philosophical questions are those questions which most of us would, upon reflection, regard as most intrinsically philosophical, or truly philosophical, or something of that sort. Some questions we surely regard as more philosophical than others, and I rather suppose that we have some philosophical questions most of us regard as the most philosophical—as most worthy, though not exclusively worthy, to be designated as philosophical. I would suggest that we probably believe, if we think about it, that these questions are classification questions which do not, at least *prima facie*, admit of true/false answers. Such questions are adjudicated on grounds such as utility and illumination, rather than truth and falsity. Accordingly then the philosophical assertion, as it is an answer to such a question, would be understood not to be a statement with a truth value, at least as 'truth value' normally tends to be understood, but a proposal, to be assessed on those criteria pertinent to proposals, whatever they might be. The suggestion then is that the philosophical assertion is actually a proposal, or normative recommendation. One supposes, of course, that the proposal is, in most cases at any rate, to be subjected to certain adequacy conditions. And it seems obvious, at least *prima facie*, that not just any proposal counts as an acceptable answer to a philosophical question, e.g., there are few philosophical questions to which "Let's shut the door" would be an acceptable answer, though perhaps an analogous proposal, "Let's forget about it," has been in fact tacitly and perhaps judiciously proposed as an answer to many philosophical questions, including the one about what is a philosophical question; forgetting about it may not be a good way to resolve practical problems, like securing enough drinking water, but it works pretty well with philosophical problems, one characteristic of which seems to be that they may be neglected with equanimity; it is not always easy to forget a philosophical problem, but it is always safe to do so; there is more than one way to stop an itch, and forgetting about it works as well as any. On the other hand let's agree, if only to see what happens, that some proposals are *better* than others. Proposals, as Quine, Carnap, and Hempel might insist, are to be assessed, at least customarily, in virtue of such criteria as simplicity, systematicity, logical elegance, etc. But would this not be another proposal on their part? A good one undoubtedly, but nonetheless a proposal? An alternative proposal regarding adequacy conditions, unattractive hopefully, is that philosophical proposals should be subjected to a criterion of "compatibility" with political or theological proposals. This is not preposterous. Some people take politics and theology more seriously than philosophy. It is also well to note that there are probably not ten hand grenades in the entire philosophical community. The "logic of proposals" has not been satisfactorily developed, but it seems clear that proposals, though lacking truth values, at least in a normal sense, are not all compatible—'compatible' being understood here in some sense other than that in which a set of statements would be compatible provided they could, in a normal sense, be conjointly true. Perhaps some notion of pragmatic compatibility is essential in unraveling these issues. Later in this essay attention is devoted to the notions of proposals and truth.

On the basis of the preceding considerations, let us say:

First-order philosophy is philosophy as proposal.

Second-order philosophy is philosophy which presupposes that the first-order questions are settled and proceeds on that basis.

WITHIN *schools* of philosophy, whether existentially or scholastically bejargoned, whether bestrewn with canonical notation or the newly endemic phrase-markers, one supposes, one hopes, that many questions can be raised and answered; surely within these schools one sees numerous examples of questions being raised and being answered, at least to the satisfaction of the individual treating the question. It seems fairly clear that the prospect of success in attacking a given problem depends on the presupposition of some notion as to what counts as a solution and how a solution may be legitimately established. Within *schools* of philosophy, where many basic questions, at least of methodology and subject matter, are closed questions, achievement would seem to be possible, and the fact that this achievement—conditional achievement perhaps—is or appears to be obtainable surely exerts a compelling fascination. I think it would be wrong to regard refuge in a school of philosophy as being simply an innocent escape from the risks of first-order philosophy, as being only the seeking of a *de facto* exit from the responsibilities of explicit axiological commitment, as being nothing more than a flight to the security of criteria and professionalism. Surely most of the truly fine philosophers of our day have belonged to one or another of these schools, attracted to it perhaps by the apparent possibility of getting something done, by the apparent possibility of bringing a reasonably honest pebble or two to the pile of human knowledge before dark. Within these schools these men have formulated remarkable contributions, without which philosophy would surely be less than it is. Indeed, when pressed by nonphilosophers, do we not point to the work of such men as indicative of what *can be* accomplished in our discipline?

On the other hand there is the philosophical country on the plains of which these schools raise their isolated platforms. It would appear to be that this is the country of decision, and that whether a platform is raised here or there is an aesthetic or, more likely, a moral choice. If even often within these schools the answer to a question must be proposal, how much more so must be the school itself; how much more so must the school itself be regarded as the institutional analogue of a human commitment, the product of a decision, the choice of a way of philosophy?

Somehow underlying the practice, and often the expression, of philosophers, there seems to be the suspicion that philosophy is a radically different sort of thing than science, whether the science be construed as formal or empirical. This notion is of course not universal. For example, there have been and still are philosophers who feel that, say, mathematical logic of scientific linguistics is peculiarly relevant to philosophy, just as there used to be people who thought this of psychology and theology, and think that the solutions to philosophical problems must somehow be effected by current theory in these areas. On the whole, however, I think that most philosophers regard philosophy as an independent discipline and that, tacitly at least, they recognize that it has its affinities not so much to formal or empirical science as to art—and that in its most philosophical moments it functions neither as empirical assertion, theorem, or dogma, but as proposal. And proposals cannot be adjudicated or tested like scientific hypotheses nor can they be examined like putative proofs within the context of a logistic system. The philosophical hypothesis, if one may use the expression, is neither analytic nor synthetic, *nor* synthetic *a priori*. It is a proposal and as such, at least *prima facie*, lacks a truth value. One is tempted to say that, disguise matters howsoever we will, philosophy remains an art, the product of a creative, disciplined imagination. Or to put it in less exalted terms, we sort of make it up as we go along.

seven

The Cognitivity Paradox I

It is a matter of definition for us that first-order philosophy is proposal. It is not a matter of definition, however, that most of what we regard as intrinsically philosophical, or most truly philosophical, *is* first-order philosophy. Also, although I do not *identify* philosophy with first *and* second-order philosophy, I do as a matter of fact regard the first- and second-order characterizations as being for most practical purposes exhaustive. Thus, when I speak of the cognitivity of philosophy, it is *not* analytic for me that philosophy consists largely of first- and second-order philosophy, though I do as a matter of fact regard that as a plausible hypothesis. If philosophy does not—substantially—consist of first- and second-order philosophy, as characterized, then this essay would appear to be significantly mistaken, perhaps fortunately, and the threat of the cognitivity paradox, to be developed, would be forestalled, or at least diminished.

The cognitivity paradox, as I shall understand

it, is one which infects all first-order philosophy, and, derivatively, all second-order philosophy. If, as I suppose, most of philosophy *is* first-order or second-order philosophy, then the cognitivity paradox would appear to be a most urgent, most serious matter for philosophical consideration. In order to help make clear the nature of the paradox I have in mind, it will be helpful, I believe, if we take this essay itself as an example of the cognitivity paradox in microcosm.

In what follows I wish to consider the cognitivity paradox in a radically simplified form, implicitly making allowance for the qualifications of the preceding paragraphs. For example, I shall speak simply of *philosophy* and trust the reader to recognize the limitations imposed on the expression. This economy allows me to present the cognitivity paradox in a form which, though admittedly simplified, should be strikingly clear.

Let us say that the thesis of this essay is:

The nature of philosophy is proposal.

We might then ask ourselves whether this thesis—presumably a philosophical assertion—is true or false. Let us suppose that it is false. Then we may dismiss it. But let us suppose it is true. If it is true, then it would seem to follow that it cannot be true. This would not mean that it would be false, but only that the assumption of its truth would lead one to deny its truth, in this case to deny that it has any truth value at all. In short, it seems that this essay wants to tell us something true about philosophy, but if what it wants to tell us is true, then it cannot be true—then it itself would be a proposal, only a proposal, and would therefore lack a truth value. And if it is only a proposal—and not a true assertion—why ought anyone to accept it? Why not accept a more comfortable proposal? But would that not be to acknowledge—at least implicitly—that the first proposal was actually true? But if one would thus acknowledge—even implicitly—that the first proposal was true, would one then not have to acknowledge—perhaps only implicitly again—*that it could not be true?*

There are a number of ways to avoid this seeming paradox. One might be to institute some sort of type distinction, or object/metalanguage distinction, which would allow me to speak of truth for my metaphilosophical assertions but not for philosophical assertions, but this solution would appear injudicious, if only because I regard myself as doing philosophy, and accordingly if there is something ultimately noncognitive about philosophy, then it is a disease, if it is a disease, which I have an obligation to contract.

Another solution would be to accept the paradox cheerfully and say, to be sure, what I offer is merely another proposal, more or less judicious, which is intended to illuminate philosophical data. As such it makes no claim to be true but merely to give us a conceptual basis for looking at philosophy from yet another direction. It itself is only proposal, only construal, and its value, if value it has, consists only in being better than many others, and perhaps in being an incitement to call forth another proposal, one more illuminating, more elegant, more satisfying.

My own approach to the matter, however, is more obnoxiously perilous.

Before presenting my solution to the cognitivity paradox perhaps it is worth saying something further about my reasons for suggesting that philosophy is essentially proposal. The best arguments, of course, are those given to the reader by himself, as he reflects on his own critical awareness of philosophy. I am led to the conclusion that philosophy is proposal largely by the obduracy of philosophical disagreement. On the other hand, even if as a matter of fact there were *no* philosophical disagreement, and never had been any, it seems it would still be the case that such disagreement *could* exist, and this is significant. Particularistic considerations such as the following have also influenced my thinking, the proposal-nature of now unpopular verifiability criteria of meaningfulness, and the apparent proposal-nature of the thesis that all necessary propositions are analytic, a thesis which is surely neither analytic in virtue of speech practice, nor a synthetic generalization presumably, nor synthetic *a priori* (in which case it would be self-refuting), which leaves us, it seems, with the alternative that it is a proposal which, with kindred proposals perhaps, offers us an illuminating and suggestive way to construe and organize a set of linguistic data, but does not deny someone else the right to reorganize linguistic data in such a way as to make room for a suitably explicated set of necessary nonanalytic propositions as, for example, Roderick Chisholm does in his book *Theory of Knowledge.* I think it is surely true that few philosophers in the past, and perhaps few today, have regarded or do regard what they are offering as the solution to philosophical problems as proposals. For example, surely the Platos, Aristotles, Hegels, and Heideggers of yesteryear and today take themselves to be propounding truths, or at least propositions which *may* be true, whether they are or not. On the other hand, since I do not know what sort of evidence, at least in crucial cases, would tend to confirm or disconfirm certain basic theses, say, the assertion of the actuality of Plato's realm of being, I am not happy speaking in terms of truth and falsity in these areas. What would it mean to call a proposition P true when one had no idea what, for example, one would take as its disconfirmation conditions? Now someone might claim, and would, that this is to presuppose some sort of empiricistic orientation which in the present case is out of order, but I do not feel it is out of order at all, and I suppose that Plato would find it as hard to convince me as I would him. And this would again suggest to me that we are not dealing with "truth" in customary senses, e.g., the sense in which it is true that all dogs are animals, or the sense in which it is true that some dogs bite. I tend to see the Platonist and the Aristotelian as proposing classificatory schemes, conceptual frameworks, etc., rather than proposing logically incompatible sets of cognitive assertions. Morever I suppose my construal of what they are doing is a *good* construal of what they are doing, *whether it is their own construal of what they are doing or not.* In this sense I could suggest that philosophy is essentially proposal, and legitimately believe that this suggestion is a well-warranted and data-illuminating suggestion, or proposal, and not be in the least deterred by the fact that all or most philosophers might not view their work in this light, if only because the illusion of stalking cosmic game is nobler fantasy than the vision of a competitive plurality of proposals, each attempting in its own way to articulate the turbulent mystery of experience.

But what of the cognitivity paradox?

Proposals are not random, though there is no logical reason why they might not be. Computers might be designed to produce random proposals, but people are not on the whole so designed. The proposals which people produce are influenced by a number of factors, and perhaps the most influential of these are psychological rather than logical. It seems reasonably clear that one's predispositions, however acquired, one's self-image, one's heroes, one's self-interests, etc., tend to affect the philosophical proposals to which one commits oneself. Such factors might even *determine* the proposals to which one commits oneself, but they presumably could not determine the set of proposals to which one *should* commit oneself. The normative question arises even within the context of a deterministic system. Analogously it might be determined that an individual would utter proposition P at a given juncture, but that he is determined to utter it does not affect its truth value. Similarly that one is determined to adopt proposal P does not determine that proposal P is the best proposal. One might well be determined to adopt an inferior proposal. Within the deterministic context, of course, presumably an individual would not be *blamed* for adopting proposal P, except perhaps by way of supplying him or others with future-regarding negative reinforcement; but it could still be said that his adoption of the proposal he did *was* a mistake—just as the uttering of a false proposition is a mistake, even though the individual were determined to utter it. In that sense then one might speak of the proposal to which he *should have* committed himself. Even within a deterministic context the normative concept is important. One reason for this is that man seems to be so constituted that, statistically at least, he seeks the better and avoids the worse, which is not to deny that what *is* the better and the worse for *him* depends on *his nature*, his own nature, man's nature and not that of god nor beast; surely it would not be surprising if given rational insight into the better—that which is better for *him*—he should find the totality of his energies felicitously rotating in its pursuit, even though he knows that the same nature which has determined what shall be his greatest good may have simultaneously determined that he shall never achieve it. If evolution has at last contrived an animal which wonders and wants to know, which seeks the truth and the good, which hopes to understand and to love before it dies, so much the better for evolution, so much the worse for the saber-toothed tiger and the pterodactyl. But such considerations complicate the argument.

Proposals, generally, tend to be held subject to certain adequacy conditions. What adequacy conditions a given proposal is subjected to may vary. Rudolf Carnap and the Chief Druid will not see eye to eye on adequacy conditions, one supposes. On the other hand, from the point of view of one set of adequacy conditions, a given proposal might well seem to be the *best*, or perhaps *not the best*, proposal available, at least at a given time. In short, if certain types of value judgments can be cognitive, it seems that a second-order or derivative cognitivity might be claimed for proposals.

In the briefest way possible let us say that if philosophical assertions are proposals, then they cannot have truth values in customary senses, such as are exhibited by claiming that all dogs are animals, or that some dogs bite. Similarly, in any customary sense, 'Let's shut the door' would not be thought to possess a truth value. On the other hand proposals can, it seems, be adjudicated as being better or worse, and it does not seem altogether absurd to think of a proposal as being the best, or the best known, at least from the point of view of a given set of adequacy conditions. Accordingly, if it can be *true or false* to say 'Proposal P is the best proposal available at time t' or, more boldly, 'Proposal P is the best proposal', then it seems we might well consider proposal P to be *cognitive*, though we might not wish to assign it a truth value. This is to extend the meaning of 'cognitive', of course, for hitherto 'x is cognitive' has been held to entail 'x possesses a truth value'. The extended concept of cognitivity would allow what one might call derivative cognitivity to proposals, provided that an associated assertion, e.g., 'Proposal P is the best proposal', was cognitive in the *strict* sense, i.e., did possess a truth value. On the other hand my own inclination in these matters, to be developed shortly, is to retain the verbal strictness of 'cognitivity' in such a way that 'x is cognitive' will still entail 'x possesses a truth value', but the concept of possessing a truth value will be extended. One hopes this will not be misleading; it is not essential to my argument; its justification is that I would like to speak of *truth* with respect to philosophical assertions, but to do so traditional concepts of truth, at least as exhibited in statements to the effect that all dogs are animals and that some dogs bite, will no longer suffice.

The cognitivity of philosophy presupposes the cognitivity of value judgments. If value judgments are noncognitive, so too is philosophy. If philosophy is proposal, and proposals can be adjudicated only in virtue of value judgments, and value judgments are noncognitive, then philosophy is noncognitive. For example, to illustrate, if noncognitivism in metaethics is a proposal to illuminate data, and the cognitivity of proposals depends on value judgments, and noncognitivism regards value judgments as noncognitive, then noncognitivism is, to put it mildly, its own worst enemy. Of course my position does not entail that *all* value judgments are cognitive. That would be an independent question. It does entail that *some* value judgments are cognitive, and would claim that at least some of these are relevant to philosophical adjudication. The ethical noncognitivist, incidentally, in an effort to escape the time bomb which he has planted in his own position, if he notices it, might be expected shortly to return to the old drawing board, that fabled bark on which we draw our distinctions, and discover some new and useful ones, perhaps ascertaining at last that at least certain crucial value judgments are cognitive whereas the others are not; and it would not be surprising if he should discover that it is his own which are of the cognitive variety and the others which are of the less estimable ilk, but only time can tell. At any rate it would seem that such a concession, permitting cognitivity to certain basic value judgments, would transform noncognitivism irreparably into a form of eclectic cognitivism, which might be hard put to defend its division of value judgments into such radically separate classes as the cognitive and the noncognitive. Surely noncognitivism would become less fun to defend if this concession were made, and when a philosophical position ceases to be fun to defend, it is on its way out. If noncognitivism would wish to retain a cognitivity claim for its own philosophical hypotheses, it would seem to have little ground for denying cognitivity to other philosophical hypotheses, at least those denying its own, for the negation of a philosophical hypothesis is itself presumably a philosophical hypothesis, and the negation of a value judgment is presumably again a value judgment; and if noncognitivism would be forced to allow cognitivity to philosophical hypotheses challenging its own, then it seems a short step to allowing cognitivity to other philosophical hypotheses, pertaining, say, to the good, to right, to moral responsibility, to how a man should live, etc. My own conviction in this matter is that value judgments can, suitably understood, be regarded as cognitive, and it is their cognitivity which bestows cognitivity on philosophy.

I think it will be granted that certain value judgments may be cognitive, relative to given objectives. For example, I think it will be granted that a given philosophical proposal might be, relative to certain adequacy conditions, the best proposal available. On the other hand, relative to another set of adequacy conditions, it might not be so regarded. This looks as though the cognitivity of these proposals then would be merely a conditional cognitivity. Whereas it is perhaps well to regard all cognitivity as conditional in some sense, for example, on the nature of man, if he has a nature, I do not think we need to let cognitivity be regarded as merely relative to given particular sets of adequacy conditions, for *sets of adequacy conditions themselves may be adjudicated.* Some are better than others.

There is, one might hope, an ideal set of adequacy conditions and, conformable to these conditions, an ideal set of philosophical proposals to account for experience. One might be willing, if one were certain that a given proposal were a member of this ultimate set, to speak not of its being a proposal, but of its being true. Accordingly one might be willing—though I do not press the point—to speak of philosophical assertions as being either true or false, and thus, if one wishes, not as being proposals at all. One might then think of oneself not as manufacturing *proposals* lacking truth values, but as *proposing* statements which are either true or false, though presumably one could not be certain which they were.

Is the notion of an ideal set of adequacy conditions, perhaps never to be explicitly articulated, unintelligible? I do not think so because it seems we can reject various sets of adequacy conditions as being nonideal, and this suggests that there might be some set of adequacy conditions which we would find *ultimately satisfying*—and which others, too, might find *ultimately satisfying*. If this is a bit of mythology, it is perhaps no worse than some others.

Let us now consider, in some detail, the possibility of ascertaining, if it exists, or inventing, if it does not, the nature of philosophical truth, particularly with respect to the possible role of ideal sets in such an ascertainment, or invention.

eight

The Cognitivity Paradox II

Would it be absurd to suppose that there might be some ideal set of adequacy conditions and, conforming to this set of conditions, an ideal set of philosophical proposals to account for experience?

Whether or not this is absurd depends obviously on whether sense can be made of the notion of ideal sets of the sort here required.

It seems to me that some sense can be made of the notion.

Before discussing methods of elucidating the concept of ideal sets, we might note that, if sense can be made of the notion, then sense can also be made of the notion of philosophical cognitivity, and accordingly of philosophical truth. And of course, if we agree to make sense of the notion, then philosophical truths will exist. For example, if we agree to make sense of the notion of a unicorn, then statements such as 'Some unicorns exist' and 'No unicorns exist' will be cognitive, and one or the other will be true. Similarly, assuming that

77

the negation of a philosophical assertion is again a philosophical assertion, then 'Philosophical Assertion A is true' and 'It is not the case that Philosophical Assertion A is true' would both be cognitive, and at least one would be true, and since both either are, or are logically equivalent to, philosophical assertions, at least one philosophical assertion would be true, from which it would follow that there is such a thing as truth in philosophy. And of course the set of true philosophical assertions, with their corresponding false negations, would be potentially infinite, and more truth than that we would not know what to do with.

For the moment, let us suppose, prior to argument, that some sense can be made of the notion of ideal sets and that philosophical truth can be explicated in terms of such sets.

If this were true, then, as suggested earlier, one might think of oneself not as manufacturing proposals lacking truth values but as proposing statements, which would either be true or false. We mentioned, however, that presumably one could not *know* whether a given statement *were* true or false. To be sure, this is a concession to fallibilism; but this concession is surely no more out of place in philosophy than in science. The interesting question is whether or not one could have good grounds for supposing that a given statement, philosophical or scientific, were true; such grounds apparently exist in science, and one supposes, similarly, that rational grounds for truth commitment do, or could, exist in philosophy, though naturally one would not expect them to be the same, or at least not completely. For example, we might be relatively sure that a given philosophical hypothesis was *not* true, would not be a member of the ideal set of philosophical assertions, if we observed that we and the rest of the philosophical community, in the light of moral, intellectual, and aesthetic considerations, tended to reject the assertion; and we might regard a given philosophical assertion as *true*, as being a member of the ideal set of philosophical assertions, if it commended itself to our moral, intellectual, and aesthetic judgment and seemed to commend itself similarly to the moral, intellectual, and aesthetic judgment of the philosophical community at large.

The foregoing is based, of course, on the assumption that certain intellectual, moral, and aesthetic requirements would be prescribed by an ideal set of adequacy conditions. This assumption, naturally, is arguable. For example, it might be suggested that aesthetic or moral considerations are irrelevant criteria for appraising philosophical assertions; similarly, though I suppose few people would take this as seriously, it might be claimed that, at this fundamental level, an appeal to our intellectual nature has no particular claim to our attention, but that an appeal to our concept of the sublime, or some such, should have priority, and that the intellect should not only accommodate itself to this commitment but should be pressed into the service of rationalizing it; more likely men would simply disagree as to what one's intellectual nature prescribed, some understanding such an appeal in terms of consistency and continuity with scientific construals, and others perhaps in terms of consistency and responsiveness to claims of human self-importance, cosmic self-image, deep-seated desires, fears, hopes, etc. Basic considerations of these sorts suggest that the attempt to explicate the concept of ideal sets and, derivatively, philosophical (and moral and axiological) cognitivity and truth may be foredoomed to failure, but they, in themselves, do not guarantee this failure and since truth, whether discovered or created, is a prize of inestimable value, one supposes, one is encouraged to address oneself with temerity and determination to the program of ascertainment or explication. I suspect it is better to have failed at this sort of thing than not to have tried it.

So then how might one go about ascertaining or explicating the notion of philosophical truth on what might be called the Ideal Set Approach?

Let us suppose that we have a linguistic entity of assertive form which we regard as philosophical. We will not regard this entity as a proposal now for we are interested in the notion of philosophical truth. We will regard it as an assertion; we will call it P. We might then attempt to explicate the notion of P's truth as follows:

P would be philosophically true if and only if P would be a member of the ideal set of philosophical beliefs.

We might then explicate the notion of the ideal set of philosophical beliefs as follows:

A set S of philosophical beliefs is the ideal set of philosophical beliefs if and only if it is the set of philosophical beliefs best conforming to the set of philosophically ideal adequacy conditions.

We might then attempt to explicate the notion of the set of philosophically ideal adequacy conditions as follows:

A set S' of philosophical adequacy conditions is the philosophically ideal set of adequacy conditions if and only if it is the set of philosophical adequacy conditions which would be fixed by an ideally rational and informed community of philosophers.

There are numerous difficulties and obscurities in this approach. It requires serious amendment and perhaps exasperated rejection. Yet I think it will be illuminating to consider it in some detail, for in spite of its shortcomings, it, or something like it, is one of the few at least initially plausible approaches to an account of philosophical truth.

To begin, it should be noted that it is neither a correspondence nor a coherence theory of truth; for in the first instance a belief would be true if and only if it *was* a member of the ideal set of philosophical beliefs, not if it corresponded with a member of the set; the relation here is identity and not correspondence; and in the second instance, whereas it is supposed that the set of ideal philosophical beliefs will be in some sense consistent ('consistency' would have to be *formally defined* without recourse to the notion of truth), consistency itself would not be the factor which would *constitute* the truth of the set of beliefs; and if consistency cannot constitute the truth of the set of beliefs, then it does not seem likely that any other purely logical relation could do so; for example, if entailment should be suggested, perhaps mutual entailment among all members of the set of beliefs, and "mere consistency" disparaged, it should be enough to point out that entailment can be reduced to "mere consistency" plus negation: for example, 'P entails Q' is logically equivalent to 'It is not the case that P and not-Q are consistent'. Further, one supposes that given data-statements are always compatible with more than one account; and there seems to be no particular reason, other than to grind metaphysical axes, to make it analytic that there can be only one exhaustive and coherent account; and even if there could be, in some sense, only one exhaustive and coherent account, presumably being exhaustive and coherent would not be what would make the account true, but its exhaustiveness and coherence would be consequences of its truth; at any rate, the above account of philosophical truth is itself *not* a coherence account.

I do not know if the preceding account would be well described as a pragmatic account. Perhaps. But I would suppose not. It seems to make truth something rather remote, something rather removed from the "cash" of everyday experience, something that may never be ascertained; moreover it does not deny the possibility that the set of ideal beliefs, as characterized, might be such that perhaps the population at large should, in the interests of benevolence, be precluded from learning them, because of their oppressive or devastating aspects; what if it turned out to be an ideal belief that man was a machine, of a cybernetic complexity of which a Lamettrie could never have dreamed; would this truth make us free? It is altogether possible that, for some minds, the human consequence of truth might be despair; if this is the case, in the interests of social hygiene, if not of human dignity, perhaps the peddling of truth should be strictly controlled, as certain despotisms have maintained; perhaps, as some of our youngsters seem to suggest, drugs are better than truth, and less dangerous; what is the point of shooting people in the soul, even if they deserve it? Truth, like fire, can burn as well as illuminate. On the other hand what truth can burn should perhaps be burned; the mind which knows itself to be mortal can perhaps better appreciate the feel of tree bark and the smell of a handful of grass; if truth can make small things great, like grass and men, that is a point in its favor. The construal does have an affinity, of course, with Peirce's account of truth, but Peirce's account, in my opinion, doesn't seem particularly pragmatic either. It is possible on my account, and on Peirce's, that a true belief might never solve a problem, work in anyone's experience, or even be discovered at all. Truth, as I propose it, would not be good for very much, except itself.

The expressions 'philosophical', 'philosophically', and 'philosophers' occur as primitives in the account. The reasons for this being the case should be fairly clear, given the first sections of this essay. There we attempted to argue that it is extremely difficult to clarify, satisfactorily, these notions, but yet that we were familiar with them, and seemed to have an intuitive grasp of their significance. Accordingly, assuming, because unable to do much else, that we have some notion of what a philosophical assertion is, we are now engaged in considering what account might be given of the truth of such assertions. Hopefully, this is something like being unable to define, satisfactorily, the expression 'man' and yet being pretty familiar with the notion, having little difficulty in recognizing things to which it is properly applied, etc., and then attempting to make sense of the notion of a certain property of some men, say, that of having red hair, possessing a driver's license, knowing little about gardening, etc. 'P is obscure' does not, presumably, entail 'P is hopelessly unintelligible', 'P is nonsense', 'P is to be forgotten about as soon as possible', etc.

Further, although adequacy conditions are often thought of in connection with proposals rather than beliefs, it seems permissible to speak of adequacy conditions for beliefs, and to hypothesize that there are conditions which a belief would have to meet before it could be regarded as well warranted, justified, or adequate by a rational and informed community. It should be noted in this connection that the empirical or analytic truth of a belief is *not* a condition for its adequacy; presumably many true beliefs do not meet satisfactory adequacy conditions, as when an individual truly believes P but on insufficient or poorly interpreted evidence; similarly some false beliefs may well meet stringent adequacy conditions, as when an individual justifiably believes P on the basis of a judicious interpretation of an abundance of relevant evidence, but yet P is false. On the other hand philosophical truth, if we wish to suppose there is such, is presumably *not* to be regarded along the lines of empirical or analytic truth, so the relation of a given philosophical assertion to its relevant adequacy conditions might be considered in a somewhat different light than the relation of its empirical and analytic counterparts to their respective adequacy conditions. Whereas it would be a mistake to regard the truth of a belief concerning the analyticity of a statement as being *constituted* by its conformity to certain adequacy conditions, it is not clear that the truth of a belief concerning philosophical matters might not judiciously be thought of as being constituted, ultimately, by its conformity to certain adequacy conditions; similarly, whereas it would be a mistake to regard the truth of a belief concerning empirical matters to be *constituted* by its conformance to certain adequacy conditions, it is well to remember that one often has, in empirical matters, a conceivable entity externally related to the belief in question, say, the nonflatness of the earth, which is at least logically discoverable; but the philosophical realm, on the other hand, does not seem to abound in such externally related, theoretically discoverable entities; accordingly it does not seem impossible that one might well think of conformance with adequacy conditions, if sufficiently ideal, as being, ultimately, a truth-making property in the case of philosophical beliefs, rather than merely being an index to likely truth, as in the case of empirical and analytic truths.

Assuming, at least for the time, that the preceding three biconditionals are intelligible, we might note that perhaps one of the most interesting questions that can be raised in connection with them pertains to their own cognitivity. How ought one to understand them, not in detail now, but more generally? Are they, themselves, best regarded as proposals, or are they best regarded as being themselves, in some sense, true? Or, of course, false?

They might be regarded as a complex conceptual proposal which, once accepted, would determine a field of philosophical truths. As such they themselves would be neither true nor false, though both truth and falsity would depend upon them. That being the case at the root of philosophy would lie three proposals and all else would be cognitive. On this approach one does not have to worry about whether or not the biconditionals would themselves be members of the set of ideal beliefs, etc. Not being beliefs but proposals they could not be members of any set of beliefs, and thus could not be members of an ideal set of beliefs. Accordingly the embarrassing logical possibility that the ideally rational and informed community might *disapprove* of the biconditionals would not *logically* affect their status as determining the field of philosophical truths. Even if, as a matter of fact, the ideal community should *reject* beliefs which might be phrased in the same terms as the above proposals, the proposals could still be maintained. Thus it could be false that a belief resembling the proposal was philosophically true, and yet be the case that the *proposal* determined philosophical truth. On the other hand, if it seems, as is possible, that a rational and informed community would *not* accept the proposals, *as proposals*, perhaps they should be discarded. One might say that if it seems plausible that a rational and informed community would reject *beliefs* statable in the same terms as the proposals, then this would suggest that the proposals are not judicious; similarly, however, if it seems a rational and informed community might actually accept *beliefs* phrased in the same terms as the proposals, this would seem to indicate that the proposals would be judicious. In short, whereas proposals and beliefs cannot be logically incompatible, obviously beliefs will condition the acceptability or nonacceptability of proposals. Thus a proposal could determine truth and it be the case that one of the truths it determined was statable in the same terms as the proposal. This involves no circularity, either vicious or benevolent, because the proposal would be fundamental. It would not logically depend on the existence of a corresponding belief. On the other hand, of course, the fact that a rational and informed community would, or would not, hold such corresponding beliefs is obviously of pragmatic relevance to the acceptability or nonacceptability of the proposal. One could, although one would not wish to, explicate truth in terms of a rational and informed community if such a community would not itself accept such an explication.

But perhaps this "proposal approach" to the biconditionals is mistaken. Perhaps it should be maintained that they are simply true, not in the sense of themselves being members of the ideal set of philosophical beliefs, but simply in virtue of their meaning. In short, perhaps one should claim that the biconditionals are analytic; that they unpack our scarcely understood but *de facto* intentions and commitments in these matters; that they make explicit for us hitherto obscured semantic and conceptual subtleties; that they spell out for us what we really *mean* when we speak of philosophical cognitivity and truth.

This is an interesting notion, and its force extends well beyond the plausibility of the preceding biconditionals, for it might well turn out that *that* set of biconditionals does *not* unpack the notions of philosophical cognitivity and truth, but yet that *some set* of biconditionals, not yet discovered, might succeed, and thus that philosophical cognitivity, seemingly incapable of rescue by the most heroic endeavors and equipment, might yet be saved by the humblest instrumentalities in the philosopher's arsenal, the meanings of his words.

But is this likely?

In philosophy, as in morals, it seems probable that no issue of interest is likely to be resolved by recourse to semantic analysis. For example, let us suppose that we have some difference of opinion with a given individual as to what is good, or right; it is unlikely that this difference of opinion is going to be resolved by telling him that he speaks English incorrectly, or does not fully understand the meanings of the words involved. International disputes, for example, are not likely to be resolved by dictionary exchange programs. Further, words, like ourselves, are transient entities, coming and going, and changing along the way. If words were really the arbiter of philosophical disputes, the tenability of philosophical solutions would be a matter of linguistic accident, relativized to given speech communities, perhaps even to the idiolects of the individuals composing these communities. If the answer to the question "What is philosophy?" truly depends on "What is the meaning of the expression 'philosophy' in English today?", then it seems the answer might well be one thing for Beowulf, another for Chaucer, another for Shakespeare, etc. Further, even if it be true that the answers to philosophical questions lie like undiscovered gold in the words about us, it is worth pointing out that we, or most of us, do not believe it; for example, most philosophers address themselves to philosophical problems by thinking about them; and not by looking things up in the dictionary, or, more plausibly, by polling carefully selected samples of native informants, presumably representing a suitable cross-section of the speech community in question. One might, of course, boldly accept the results of one's own idiolectical intuitions as decisive on these matters. There is much to be said for this approach. It is simpler and speedier than science, and it is also less expensive.

If one can distinguish between things and their names, or between things and words, and I suppose we can, then it seems one can distinguish, and should, between an investigation of things and an investigation of their names, or between an investigation of things and an investigation of words. Let us suppose that we have a complex x which we will call 'science' and a complex y which we will call 'philosophy'. Let us also assume that we can tell them apart, much as we can tell giraffes from zebras, or trees from cars, or kindness from cruelty, or listening to music from playing chess. Then it might seem rather unimportant to us, though it would probably be justifiably important to a philologist, that one happened to be called 'science' and the other 'philosophy'. Let us suppose, analogously, that someone is extremely interested in the nature and habits of elephants, can recognize them, goes about studying them, etc. As far as he is concerned, it would make no difference if the creatures in which he is interested were called 'antelopes'. If they were, of course, then he would be interested not in elephants but in antelopes, those huge, thick-skinned, flexible-snouted, almost hairless, twin-tusked, mammalian things, but he would still be interested in the same thing he was before. Analogously, one supposes that there is such a thing as philosophy, to be distinguished from such a thing as science, which deserves, and has received and will receive, intellectual consideration, regardless of the name we call it. The claim that there is such a *thing* as philosophy, and that its nature is a fit object for inquiry, and that its nature does not depend on linguistic conventions, as would the meanings of words, does not, incidentally, commit one to a doctrine of immutable essences or fixed natures, or something of that sort, any more than the zoologist's belief that there are elephants commits him to a belief that the theory of evolution is false; if elephants can evolve, there is no reason to deny the privilege to philosophy; perhaps that is just another one of those things which philosophy and elephants have in common. And of course if the nature of elephants, or, say, antelopes, can present problems, why not the nature of complex human phenomena like philosophy and science? "What is philosophy?" and "What is science?" are not only obscure, vague, irritating, perhaps-best-left-unasked questions; but they are also difficult questions. But whatever sort of questions they are, they are presumably not to be decided by semantic inquiry; analogously, elephants have the last say on the nature of elephants, not the dictionary.

If I have been successful to this point, by now one suspects, if one was not already convinced, that philosophical questions are not likely to be resolved by finding out about the meanings of words. This is not to deny, of course, that some clarification of meaning might be a precondition of philosophical success, insofar as it can be achieved, which is probably not far. It is not always a well-warranted assumption that one knows what one is talking about; but neither, too, is it always a well-warranted assumption that one never knows what one is talking about unless one can produce reportive definitions at the drop of a gauntlet.

On the other hand let us suppose that we regarded it as plausible that the meanings of our words, as we now *implicitly* understand and use them, *are* decisive with respect to issues connected with philosophical cognitivity and truth; that the meanings of our words, if we rightly understood them, would, once and for now, resolve these complex issues. Even if we believed this, it would behoove us to be cautious. Linguists, for example, who are presumably the professionals in the areas of language, whereas philosophers are the amateurs, tend to be staggered at the problems involved in ascertaining meaning; for example, it is not so clear that the notion of having a meaning or being meaningful is an altogether intelligible notion; meaning has been discussed in terms ranging from stimulus and response to semantic universals, which seem to be innate ideas under another name. Linguists tend to be more comfortable with questions of phonology; and perhaps, more hazardously, those of morphology; and, one gathers, in the next century, or so, something of preliminary importance may be done with the questions of semantics. This is not to recommend that philosophers leave semantic analysis to the professionals, though I think there is perhaps a little something to be said for that recommendation (not much), but merely to suggest that since the concept of meaning and the apparatus for the determination of meaning still wobble in limbo, that one ought not to be too sanguine about establishing that one meaning analysis or another is the correct one for 'philosophical truth'. Beyond this general point, there will presumably also be difficulties as to what to do about vagueness and nonuniformity of usage. For example, what set of logically possible entities falls within the application range of the expression 'man'? What if native speakers disagree on the application range of expressions? What sorts of natives qualify as acceptable native informants? What percentages of the speech population would have to be in substantial agreement before one could speak seriously of the meaning of an expression E in some language L? There are many problems involved in linguistic investigations which are *not* empirical, though of course the answers to empirical questions will vary depending on how they are resolved.

One of the most interesting objections to the notion of assuming that some biconditionals of the sort in question are analytic is that there seems to be no way of discriminating between the hypotheses:

H_1: Meaning M is now, and was, the meaning of expression E.

H_2: Meaning M is now, but was not before, the meaning of expression E.

In short, meaning might alter or develop under investigation. Linguistic investigation might not discover meaning so much as create it.

Let us suppose we have a native informant and we begin to question him about the possible application range of an expression, say, 'man'. Suppose, at the end of our investigation, after describing various entities to him, drawing pictures, etc., we have a fairly clear hypothesis as to what he takes to be its meaning. The question would then arise as to whether this is what he *meant all along,* as to whether this nice meaning was really there, invisible so to speak, and was merely elicited by us, or whether instead, in the course of the investigation, he *decided* what he would mean by 'man'. One becomes suspicious of the claim that such and such is what was *really meant all along;* perhaps what is discovered is what the individual is *now willing to mean* by the expression. The dangers of this sort of thing would seem to be particularly perilous in questions dealing with complex expressions. For example, suppose someone claims that the preceding biconditionals are analytic. Is it likely that they were what he *really* meant; or would it not be more likely that they now just seem to him such that he is satisfied to regard them as analytic, as what he had really meant? How would he know that they are what he had really meant? Claiming that they are what he really had meant might be only a way of fooling himself into the belief that he is not merely, unbeknownst to himself, engaged in manufacturing linguistic proposals. As a last point here, it might be suggested that it is likely that more than one hypothesis as to the meaning of a given expression will always be compatible with the native informant's responses, and his own thinking on these matters, and, accordingly, that within circumscribed limits, the linguist's hypothesis as to the meaning of the expression will be a matter of choice. If this is true, as it seems to be, then it would appear to be incorrect to claim that one could empirically *establish* the meanings of words, though of course this is not to deny that many hypotheses as to the meaning of words might be empirically rejected; it is only to claim that it is probable that they could not all be rejected except one, which would then be *the* meaning. This phenomenon would appear to be a subcase of the general point that it always seems possible to illuminate the same set of data by means of more than one account or explanation.

If the preceding argumentation is, substantially, correct, then it seems that it would be a matter of choice whether one would say, of a set of biconditionals relevant to philosophical cognitivity and truth, that they articulated what one had meant by these notions, or that they articulated what one had *now* decided to mean by these notions. In the first case the biconditionals would be supposed to be true, and analytic; in the second they would be considered stipulative proposals, and would not be thought to possess truth value. Whereas it is, one supposes, a matter of choice between these alternatives, this is not to say that the choices would be equally judicious. It seems to me more honest and plausible to limit one's claim to the incontestable assertion that one had *now* decided to regard philosophical cognitivity and truth in the light of the biconditionals. It seems a very dubious hypothesis that whatever now seems right to someone must be what he implicitly had in mind all along. This is something like saying that the poem or the picture that the artist produces and is satisfied with must be somehow or other a faithful articulation or copy of a hitherto undisclosed poem or picture. Plato himself would probably not put a drachma on that hypothesis. Incidentally, it is not altogether clear that hypotheses of this sort are even empirically meaningful; but one supposes they are; it seems one can imagine that someday in the future such hypotheses might be testable; perhaps brain-scanners will be available and correlations worked out between microstates of the brain at time t_1 and, at time t_2, events such as philosophies and poems and plays, and the producing entity's psychological sense of having "gotten it right." At such a time, or under such conditions, perhaps the bold hypothesis that the biconditionals are analytic, at least for a given individual, would be testable. In the meantime one might say that one didn't know, but that the hypothesis seemed implausible.

On the other hand, if one *does* regard the meanings of words as being decisive in matters of this sort, one should not be encouraged to abandon semantic inquiry, for it would seem incredible that the expressions 'philosophical cognitivity' and 'philosophical truth' have no meaning. Surely we tend to use them in a nonrandom fashion, seldom make grammatical mistakes in sentences containing them, etc. These facts, of course, do not guarantee that a word has a meaning; they might be explained in virtue of such things as the morphological transformations governing certain word classes plus the acknowledged *denotative* value of such related expressions as 'philosophy' and 'philosophical question'. I have just invented the expression 'political truth' and I have nothing clearly in mind which it might mean; but I feel I could use the expression according to the rules of English, and, further, that I might use it with judicious and discriminating ease, given my familiarity with the uses of 'truth' in empirical and analytic truth, and my familiarity with the uses of 'political' in constructions such as 'political entity', 'political figure', 'political speech', etc. And it seems to me that 'political truth' would certainly *sound* meaningful; and it also seems to me that I could probably *give* it some useful meaning. Perhaps the case is analogous with 'philosophical truth'? Perhaps the words come before the meanings. Perhaps we talk first and decide what we mean second. Perhaps this is the only way to say something new.

At any rate suppose that we confront a given set of biconditionals which purport to illuminate the nature of philosophical cognitivity and truth. Now whether we regard this set as analytic *or* as judicious proposals will often depend on *similar* considerations. For example, in the light of certain considerations we might be led to say that the set of biconditionals was *not*, could not have been, what we had intended and meant all along; similarly the same considerations might lead us to say that the set of biconditionals, as proposals, did *not* afford us a judicious characterization of, say, what we wanted to regard as philosophical truth. In short, for the time, let us consider the preceding biconditionals *without* raising the question of their own cognitivity. Their consideration can be, I suspect, illuminating independently of that question.

nine

The Cognitivity Paradox III

It should be recognized, of course, that specifying ultimate philosophical cognitivity in this rather counterfactual fashion, namely, in terms of the adequacy conditions and judgments best conforming to them which would be determined by an ideally rational and informed community of philosophers, does not preclude the possibility that such an ideal community might, conceivably, arrive at irreducibly incompatible adequacy conditions and conforming judgments. There is no guarantee that such an informed and rational community would tend to fix opinion in any unanimous fashion. Surely one does not wish to make it analytic that the community would not both be rational and informed if a unanimous opinion was not fixed. I do not think we know what set of opinions an ideally rational and informed community would tend to fix, or even that such a community would tend to a single fixity of opinion. As a matter of fact it is not known that such a community would even tend to a plurality of fixities, but might continue to oscillate indefinitely, never fixing an opinion or even sets of differing opinions. In the first case, where such a community would tend to a plurality of fixities, one might claim that any philosophical assertion which would occur in at least one fixed set would be true, even if its negation occurred in another fixed set, which would allow for the simultaneous truth, in this sense we are developing, of an assertion and its negation. On the other hand this would extend the concept of truth beyond the point I am willing to extend it, and I have already extended it perhaps too far. Accordingly I should like to say that if the ideally rational and informed community is one which would either tend to a plurality of fixities or would not tend to a fixity of opinion at all, then the notion of objective cognitivity in philosophy is lost, at least as far as this approach is concerned. It should be noted incidentally that this search for objective cognitivity is founded at least significantly on the desire to say that there is *truth*, in some sense, in matters moral, axiological, and philosophical, even though it admits we can never be certain that we have determined what it is. That there is *truth*, in some sense, in these matters is, I suggest, something which most of us wish to say; and accordingly my proposals in this regard are intended to provide one possible account of what might be taken to be the nature of this truth.

There is, of course, something counterintuitive about making philosophical truth dependent on the opinions of an ideally informed and rational community, even assuming that such a community would tend to fixity of opinion. There would, for example, appear to be no contradiction in the conjunction 'P is a member of the ideally fixed set of opinions and P is false'. But this would be to construe falsity in philosophy along lines other than are suggested in this essay. To be sure, there does *not appear* to be a contradiction in the following conjunction: 'That the earth is flat is an opinion which would be fixed by an ideally rational and informed community but the earth is not flat'. This is, one supposes, no more a contradiction than 'Jones thinks the earth is flat but the earth is not flat'. In the philosophical case, however, we do *not* have empirical truth conditions for philosophical assertions; for example, we do not have something like the nonflatness of the earth at hand to help us get our opinions in order. And if it is true that moral, axiological, and philosophical truth must be explicated in terms other than analytic and empirical truth, then the fact that it does not *appear* to be a contradiction to link 'P is a member of the ideally fixed set of opinions' and 'P is false' does not show that it is *not* a contradiction. Of course, as we have set things up, provided that a rational and informed community *would tend* to a fixity of opinion, it *would*, on our account, be a contradiction to link the two assertions. We are supposing that such an ideally rational and informed community would *determine* truth in such matters. Whether this is a judicious proposal or not is an independent question.

One thing that seems quite plausible is that the community in question might well be required to have virtues over and above knowledge and rationality; it would be desirable that it would have at least a bit of love as well. Probably one would not want to define such things as moral, axiological, and philosophical truth in terms of the agreement of a community which for all practical purposes might consist of mere problem-solving cybernetic mechanisms; one would hardly care to relinquish the determination of moral, axiological, and philosophical truth to such machines, even if they happen to be sentient, even if they happen to appear men; if man himself should be a machine, he is at least more than such a machine for his circuitry is ennobled by emotion and the capacity for concern.

Perhaps a more serious objection, because less easy to meet by amending or qualifying the notion of the community, would be that if we accept this proposal, we must exclude *ourselves* as being the ultimate arbiter of philosophical truth. We would have to admit that we might *firmly believe* a philosophical judgment P to be true and yet *be wrong*, because the judgment would *not* be a member of the ideally fixed set of judgments. In practice, of course, we would suppose that our judgment *would be* a member of the ideally fixed set. But in theory we would have to admit that we could be wrong. That takes a lot of admitting, and it is not easy to do, not in the heart—particularly if truth is linked to the notion of ideal opinion. It is not unlikely that we would feel that it would be at least *possible* that we would be right and the ideally fixed opinion *wrong*. This of course would *not* be possible if the truth in these matters were *determined* in virtue of the ideal opinion; we would then simply be wrong. But the fact that we might *feel* that we could be right and the ideal opinion wrong suggests that, for us, it might not be judicious to *define* the rightness and wrongness in these matters in terms of the opinion of others, howsoever ideally informed and rational—or charitable. If one does feel this way, then it would seem to be up to one to provide an alternative account of philosophical truth, which is *not* opinion-dependent, and which does, of course, allow that someone, even oneself, may be mistaken, may make an error, may believe something which is false.

I am, it is evident, I suppose, not altogether satisfied with the account of philosophical truth I have discussed in this essay, but I wish to allow that there is such a thing as philosophical truth, and thus I have set myself the problem of proposing a sense in which such truth could exist. Two further small points might well be noted here.

First, it might be suggested that the supposition of a single ideal arbiter would be preferable to the notion of the supposition of an ideally rational and informed community, for the arbiter would presumably not be plagued with incompatible pluralities of fixities, as might be a community; though of course he, like the community, might never tend to a fixed opinion. My primary reason for preferring the notion of a community to that of an arbiter is simply that it seems to me that such things as moral, axiological, and philosophical truth are best construed as being community-dependent rather than individual-dependent, howsoever ideal the individual might be. Moreover, the notion of continuing moral investigation, philosophical inquiry, etc., seems to me more reassuring when a community is presupposed; perhaps because of the give-and-take of opinion and conviction; thus, if this is to democratize the criteria for significant truths, it is in my opinion at least preferable to autocratizing it. Incidentally, I have spoken occasionally, it might be noted, of not only philosophical but of moral and axiological truth. This is not a conflation nor an oversight of some sort, but a reflection of my suspicion that a successful analysis of, or explication of, the notion of philosophical truth would be much akin to that which would serve for moral or axiological truth. In a sense both moral and philosophical truth might be regarded as species of axiological, or valuational, truth. The construals or proposals in these other cases, of course, would be somewhat different. Common elements would presumably involve the notion of adequacy conditions and communities which would be, at least, rational and informed.

Secondly, that the ideal community here presupposed will never exist in fact does not affect its utility as the determinant of philosophical truth. Just as it might be true or false to say 'If I had struck the match, it would have lit', in spite of the fact that I did not and can never strike the match, so it might be true or false to say 'If an ideal community existed, it would believe that the earth was round', or 'If an ideal community existed, it would fix as the set of its opinions the following . . .'. And of course this sort of thing would be true or false even if the world were to be destroyed tomorrow, as it may be. It is no part of these proposals that the ideal community be realized in time; indeed, it is an assumption of the proposals that it could not be; to claim that the ideal community was realized at a time t would be, ruling out the plurality-of-fixities and the indefinite-vacillation possibilities, to claim implicitly that philosophical truth was then known and that, subject to the community remaining at its current level of, say, rationality and information, its set of philosophical opinions and judgments would never alter; similarly a claim would be involved that the community in question could not be better informed or more rational. All of these claims would seem dubious if lodged on behalf of any actually existing community, at least any community that we find it easy to conceive of as actually existing at a given historical time. There is, of course, nothing logically impossible about the actual existence of an ideal community; its existence would only be empirically improbable. It might also be noted that even should the ideal community exist for a given time, there is no reason to suppose that it would continue to exist. It might become less ideal with the passage of time, not even realizing and being incapable of knowing that it had once embodied the ideal; or, of course, it might be destroyed by less rational or informed but more technologically advanced neighbors; it is, after all, one thing to know how to build a musket or hydrogen bomb and another thing to build one; and still another to use one; perhaps such a community, incredibly enough, might even allow itself to be destroyed in order to effect the moral reform of its neighbors; who knows how such a community would conceive of such matters; who knows how it would act? To be sure, one might ask if all this makes any sense. Certainly there would be numerous problems in specifying criteria which would be satisfied by an ideal community. But one supposes that these problems would not be absolutely or completely insurmountable, nor render the notion of such a community unintelligible. Perhaps one could only approximate the criteria for an ideal community, but even this would make the notion intelligible and useful, at least to some significant degree. Surely we know something about what it is to be rational and informed, and to care about things.

On the other hand it seems to me that there remain certain basic objections to the entire program of explicating philosophical cognitivity and truth in terms of ideal beliefs and ideal communities. The first objection is a quite general one, to the effect that it seems doubtful that the notion of truth could ever be satisfactorily explicated in terms of belief, howsoever well warranted or ideal the belief might be. For example, it seems to be the case that an assertion to the effect 'A believes P' entails 'A regards P as true', and if this is the case, it would appear that 'true' could not be explicated in terms of belief without circularity. In brief, one would not wish to explicate 'P is true' in terms such as 'P would be a member of the ideal set of beliefs' because 'P would be a member of the ideal set of beliefs' presumably entails 'P would be a member of the set of beliefs ideally to be regarded as *true*'. Thus 'true', to be explicated or defined, in the explicandum or definiendum, would covertly occur in the explicans or definiens. For the explicans or definiens to perform its function, one should be able to make sense of the notion of belief without recourse to the notion of truth. It would not be illuminating to be told, in effect, that 'P is true' meant 'P is believed to be true', or something along these lines. A related but less general objection to the program of explicating philosophical cognitivity and truth in terms of ideal beliefs and ideal communities is as follows: Supposing that we do accept that, from our point of view, what makes a philosophical assertion true is that it would be an assertion fixed by the ideal community, what then would make a philosophical assertion true *from the standpoint of the ideal community?* What would one *then mean* by philosophical truth? Would one really mean only that it was believed, and that that was sufficient to make it true? It seems that our approach to truth would not work *for the ideal community;* and, of course, if it would not work for the ideal community, there seems to be no special reason for looking on it with much favor ourselves. It would be like saying, what makes P true is that Jones believes it; but one hopes that Jones, at least, does not believe that.

Do these considerations demolish the possibility of establishing some useful notion of philosophical cognitivity and truth in terms of ideal communities? I do not think so, but one would have to be far bolder than one has been. Perhaps some radical analysis of belief might be required, perhaps in terms of behavior, or Peircean rules of action, or something of this sort. Also it seems one would have to speak not simply of those beliefs which were fixed by an ideal community, but those beliefs which would *satisfy* an ideal community. The true belief would then be that which an ideal community would find satisfactory. Upon reflection, I do not think that this is altogether counterintuitive. For example, if we choose to believe that human beings have inalienable rights, a philosophical belief, one supposes, would we really say that this is *true* because, as a matter of fact, they *do have* some unusual sort of nonempirical entities, inalienable rights? How would we test that claim? It seems more plausible to say that it is *true* that human beings have inalienable rights because it *satisfies us profoundly* to act toward human beings in certain ways, perhaps to regard them as ends and never solely as means, or something along these lines. Thus in saying that human beings have inalienable rights perhaps one is saying that one should behave towards them, in certain circumstances, as though one cared for and respected them—and a reason for supposing this to be *true* would be that it seemed to us profoundly satisfying to do so. But one wishes to allow that one may be mistaken, and so one allows the possibility that a principle might satisfy us profoundly and yet be false. Accordingly the search for justice, etc., might be well regarded as the search for those principles in terms of which an *ideal community would be profoundly satisfied to act*. One hopes, of course, that one's own judgments and actions, those which most satisfy one, would be those approved by an ideal community; and insofar as this hope is well warranted, one might even conceive oneself as being, to a small extent, a participant in such a community; an analogy here along Platonic lines would be the relation of the irregular but roundish earthbound form to the Platonic circle; it is not identical with the Platonic circle but to some extent it participates in its form, indicating what could be but in our world is not; similarly one might think of one's limited and finite self as not being utterly alien to a higher self, which might be almost unrecognizable but yet would have continuity with our being and take its place in a community of higher selves. Perhaps it is to be too paradoxical but one might think of one's truest self being the self which one can never be, that one is most essentially what one is not, what one can never achieve, that of which one is forever foredoomed to fall short.

Beyond all this stumbling talk of ideal communities, beliefs, sets, analyticities, proposals, objections, and counterobjections, there looms the conviction that value judgments can be cognitive; that given the multiplex potentialities that are the nature of man, that some are better than others, and should be sought and others rejected; that there exists that which we would find ultimately satisfying, and that perhaps it is something which others, too, might find so.

That the value judgment can be cognitive cannot be well argued, for it is hardly an argument to point out that we cannot believe it to be otherwise; and indeed perhaps some of us can so believe, even in our hearts as well as in our mouths, and in our published writings; I do not know; I cannot, or at least do not seem now to be able to do so. If the value judgment can be cognitive, I think this gives us a key, as yet incompletely formed and scarcely understood, to moral, axiological, and philosophical truth. That the value judgment is cognitive seems to me in the final analysis to be incontestable and unarguable; that it is cognitive seems to me to be the result of a *recognition*, or seeing or intuition if you like, which can have no other validation than its own coercive incapacity to be humanly denied; and that such judgments can be cognitive seems to me to give evidence to the putatively obsolete claim now apparently restored more powerfully than ever that intuition, or vision, lies at the root of morality, of philosophy, of man. No man has died for the propositions of physics; but men have died for the vision that it is good to seek such truths; I think they were right; thus I think that the belief for which they died was true.

One looks upon philosophy and wonders what has become of it. Perhaps in the coming centuries it will become a type of intellectual chemistry in which, on the basis of numerous presuppositions, the laborious analysis of compounds may proceed, and thus an inventory of conditional knowledge may be accumulated; and we will witness the triumph of the scale and the measuring stick, and one will learn to sing the glories of the retort and crucible and equation. And perhaps tomorrow when the philosophical lexicon is completed and the geography of our hearts has been adequately charted and men forget philosophy and their children no longer learn her name, it may occur to someone to set a marker by man's road, in memory of what once burned upon its stones. This should be a plain marker, bearing no inscription, that it may more easily be ignored. It will mark the common grave of Plato and Spinoza; of St. Thomas and Maimonides; it will reconcile Hume and Kant, shelter the bones of anxious Sartre and proud Russell; in its dust will mingle Jews and Greeks, Englishmen and Arabs, Hindus and Frenchmen and Germans; kings and saints, and emperors and slaves. If there were to be an inscription on that stone, one might suggest a line not uncommon on certain graves along the Appian Way, the graves of unimportant men, gladiators and slaves: *Non Sum*, I am not. It would be philosophy's last smile, her last paradox.

But one may not read the signs of the future aright; after all, if someone tells you he is dead, it is not impossible that he is lying; philosophy is patient; she has a long time, and it would be a mistake to regard the coastlines of this afternoon as determining tomorrow's shape of continents. In philosophy substance has awakened; it wonders about itself and proposes to itself the assuagements of speculation. In twenty centuries it has barely opened its eyes, and has not yet begun to see.

Perhaps it is nonsense to speak of the set of philosophical assertions which would be equal in grandeur to the wonder that has aroused them. Perhaps one should speak only of proposals, and forget the notion of extending the concept of truth. It is perhaps *best* to do so. Yet there is still the lure of

115

that remote, presumably inaccessible ideal, an ideal in terms of which, apart from notions of empirical and analytic truth, one might explicate notions of moral and axiological, of philosophical truth, in terms of man's humanity itself, or his possible humanity, humanity as it might be; in terms of what would ultimately satisfy him, ultimately impress him as imperative to accept.

But enough of this.

Let us say simply that the cognitivity of philosophy seems to be proposal-dependent, and that proposals are normally thought to lack truth values, and accordingly that philosophy's self-construal as cognitive, lacking a truth value, is noncognitive. It is then suggested that proposals may have derivative cognitivity from the cognitivity of value judgments, for example, that P, a proposal, would count as cognitive provided the assertion, say, 'P is the best proposal' is cognitive. But that the cognitivity of value judgments may itself be proposal-dependent complicates the issue. Is it merely another proposal that such judgments can be cognitive? Perhaps, but if it is the *best* proposal, then what? And so hierarchies begin to ache upward, and one feels that a decision of passion must be made, that one must choose. So one chooses for cognitivity. And wonders if one has made the *best* choice. And this wondering convinces him that he has, for it shows him that he is committed to the cognitivity of value judgments, that this proposal is forced on him, that he finds it imperative to accept, and that he may thus, if he wishes, regard it as true.

So shall we say that the upshot of the foregoing is a proposal, or not? It is at least a recommendation to philosophers that they have the courage to commit themselves to the cognitivity of value judgments, in order by their own bootstraps to restore the cognitivity which they, in their official flight from the value judgment, have abandoned in word but have continued to proclaim in deed.

So now everything is just the same except that it is all different.